and Schooling

The Explorations in Feminism Collective

Kythe Beaumont
Jane Cholmeley
Claire Duchen
Renate Duelli-Klein
Catherine Itzin
Diana Leonard
Caroline Waller

Gender and Schooling

A study of sexual divisions in the classroom

Michelle Stanworth

Hutchinson
in association with
The Explorations in Feminism Collective
affiliated to the
Women's Research and Resources Centre

London Melbourne Sydney Auckland Johannesburg

Hutchinson & Co. (Publishers) Ltd

An imprint of the Hutchinson Publishing Group

17–21 Conway Street, London W1P 6JD

Hutchinson Group (Australia) Pty Ltd
30–32 Cremorne Street, Richmond South, Victoria 3121
PO Box 151, Broadway, New South Wales 2007

Hutchinson Group (NZ) Ltd
32–34 View Road, PO Box 40–086, Glenfield, Auckland 10

Hutchinson Group (SA) (Pty) Ltd
PO Box 337, Bergvlei 2012, South Africa

First published by Women's Research and Resources Centre Publications Collective 1981
© Michelle Stanworth 1981
This edition first published 1983
© Michelle Stanworth 1983
Reprinted 1983

Set in Century Schoolbook

Printed in Great Britain by The Anchor Press Ltd
and bound by William Brendon & Son Ltd,
both of Tiptree, Essex

British Cataloguing in Publication Data
Stanworth, Michelle
Gender and schooling.—(Explorations in feminism)
1. Sexism   2. Schools
I. Title   II. Series
370.19′345   LB3407

ISBN 0 09 151161 5

Contents

Acknowledgements

I wish to express my thanks to the teachers and pupils who took part in the study, and were so generous with their time and so candid in their comments. Mary McIntosh, Leonore Davidoff, Dennis Marsden, Diana Leonard and Veronica Held provided inspiration, valuable advice and encouragement. The Cambridge Women and Education Group sharpened my concern for the practical problems of educational change. Special thanks are due to David Held, both for his support and for his careful reading and criticism of the manuscript.

Foreword

As a feminist and sociologist with eleven years experience as a teacher in further education, I was and am concerned with the ways in which gender structures classroom interactions. We know the outcome of schooling in terms of the sexual distribution of attainment. We know also that girls may follow a similar curriculum to boys and yet emerge from school with the implicit understanding that the world is a man's world, in which women take second place. But we need to ask ourselves: what part do we as teachers play in this process? And what steps can we take to transform the impact of schooling on gender divisions?

The discussion and research that follows represents my attempt to come to terms with these questions. The study is divided into two parts: the first part aims to establish the significance of gender in relation to schooling, and to outline the importance of the struggle against sexism in education. The second part documents the empirical research that was undertaken. I have tried throughout to make the sociological analysis of education accessible to readers, because of my conviction that gender inequality in education is not merely a 'theoretical' or 'academic' concern: it is a fundamental issue, and one with which every member of our society should be familiar.

Since the research which forms the basis of *Gender and Schooling* was completed, there have been gains and losses for women and girls in terms of educational opportunity. On the positive side, more girls are enrolling for examinations in chemistry, physics and mathematics; home economics, and craft, design and technology are more often available to pupils of both sexes; and women are gaining ground in higher education. Our understanding of the impact of gender divisions on classroom practice has expanded remarkably, and teachers have begun the challenging task of revising the school curriculum so that it less often excludes, ignores or trivialises women and their concerns.

On the negative side, women make up less than one-fifth of young people on day-release courses; they have lost ground where cutbacks in educational expenditure (in teacher training, for example, or TOPs courses oriented towards typing and clerical skills) have reduced opportunities in traditional areas of female expertise. In mixed schools, boys still command the lion's share of teachers' attention (especially by posing problems for classroom control) and teachers draw back, for fear of alienating boys, from using materials that capture girls' imagination and expand their horizons. Progress has been made towards overcoming gender inequality in schools. But it must be said with equal emphasis that there is still a long way to go.

Michelle Stanworth
Cambridge
1983

References for Foreword

Gains and losses in educational opportunities for women are documented in: Equal Opportunities Commission, *Sixth Annual Report 1981*, HMSO (1982), pp. 14–15, 49–61.

Our understanding of the impact on gender divisions of classroom practice and of the curriculum owes much to several recent publications: Rosemary Deem (ed), *Schooling for Women's Work*, Routledge & Kegan Paul (1980); Sara Delamont, *Sex Roles and the School*, Methuen (1980); Alison Kelly (ed), *The Missing Half*, Manchester University Press (1981); Dale Spender, *Invisible Women*, Writers and Readers Publishing Cooperative (1982); Dale Spender and Elizabeth Sarah (eds), *Learning to Lose*, The Women's Press (1980).

PART I

INTRODUCTION:

EDUCATION AND SOCIAL INEQUALITY

That our schools welcome children impartially, that without regard for ascribed characteristics (social class, for example, or race or sex) schools stimulate individual talents to the full and reshuffle children according to ability is one of the most cherished myths of our time — the myth of meritocracy. Against this view, the overwhelming evidence is that our education system — like that of many other countries — favours those who are already privileged, and puts further obstacles in the path of those who are disadvantaged. *Origins and Destinations*,* a recent survey of 8,529 males who were educated in England and Wales, testifies to the powerful influence of socio-economic background on educational attainment. Boys whose fathers held professional, senior technical or managerial posts were three times more likely than those whose fathers were manual workers to win a grammar school place; they were five times more likely to attain 'O' levels or equivalent qualifications, ten times more likely to be in full-time education at the age of 18, and 11 times more likely to attend university. Thus those who hoped that the reforms which followed the 1944 Education Act would ensure a society in which selection was based on merit rather than social position have been disappointed; neither educational expansion nor educational reform has ushered in an era of equal opportunity.

The vision of equal opportunity which underpinned meritocratic dreams deserves to be elaborated. The promise of meritocracy was never the promise of equality (of access for everyone to resources that determine health and happiness, and to decision-making processes that govern social life), but merely the promise of a super-competitive society in which inequality would be allocated according to ability. Thus it is not surprising that meritocratic arguments never embraced women as wholeheartedly as men; for unique abilities in the realm of childcare and housework have been attributed to women, talents which "justified" the exclusion of all but the most academic of women from the hurly-burly of competition with men. Nor is it surprising that in the satirical novel *The Rise of the Meritocracy* with its devastating critique of meritocratic principles, it is women who band together to spearhead political revolt. Faced with a drift towards selective breeding, and entrenched discrepancies of power between those with "merit" and those without, feminists of the year 2034 "protest against the standards, those of achievement, by which men assess each other"; women reject a social order which, they suspect, has been constructed "expressly for the convenience of the opposite sex".

*For details of articles and books mentioned in Part I, see note 6 on pp. 61–2.

In the late 19th and early 20th centuries, policies for the education of girls and women developed (as Carol Dyhouse and Anna Davin argue) against a backdrop of fears about the "physical deterioration" of the British people. The wish that women — especially those from the working class — would devote their lives to domestic duties as servants, and as wives and mothers, was translated into a school curriculum designed to ensure that very outcome. In the context of British imperialism, women were exalted as the "guardians of the race"; but the education of those guardians was to be far less rigorous, less focussed upon scientific and technical skill, and more bounded by domestic concerns, than that of men. Ideologies concerning the separate destinies of girls and boys continued to haunt educational policy statements even after the second world war; as late as 1963, when 30 per cent of married women were in paid employment, marriage was characterised by the Newsom Report as girls' "most important vocational concern". Current statistics show that policies for gender-differentiated education continue to be reflected in the sexual distribution of attainment.

During the past decade, girls have overtaken boys in some areas; a higher proportion of girls now attempt CSE or GCE 'O' level examinations, and fewer of the female candidates fail. Girl school-leavers were, in the year 1976-77, slightly more likely than boys to attain one or two passes in GCE 'A' level subjects. On the other hand, a higher proportion of boys than girls left school with three GCE 'A' levels (9.5 and 7.1 per cent respectively), and this at a time when increasingly, entry to university courses required three good 'A' levels. Only 14,800 girls left school with suitable qualifications for university entry (three or more higher grade qualifications at 'A' level), while 21,200 boys were so qualified. Moreover, cutbacks in teacher training — where women pre-dominated, and where candidates with two 'A' levels were often accepted — have further reduced the likelihood that girl school-leavers will be equipped to go on to higher education.

Conventional measures of educational inequality such as these tend, however, to focus attention on that minority of the population who reach the upper levels of the education hierarchy. The oft-cited fact that similar proportions of women and men now gain two 'A' levels is cold comfort when we consider the majority of women — doubly handicapped by social class position as well as gender — who, lacking any marketable qualifications, end up combining unskilled and poorly-rewarded occupations with the responsibilities of housework and child care. According to the *General Household Survey 1977*, among "economically active" adults, 49 per cent of men, but 60 per cent of women, possessed no educational qualifications whatsoever. They were joined in 1976-77 by 52,770 girls (over 14 per cent of female school-leavers) who entered employment without a single pass in CSE or GCE subjects.

These girls and women will be severely disadvantaged when it comes to holding their jobs in times of increasing unemployment. They face (assuming they maintain employment) a greater sexual disparity in earnings which denies to many of them a tolerable living wage: women in full-time manual employ-ment in October 1979 had average weekly earnings of £58.24, while their male counterparts earned £96.94. Moreover, if recent trends continue, there will be fewer opportunities for women who are unqualified than for men to upgrade their employment prospects. Over all, the numbers of apprenticeships available to women are few, and their range highly circumscribed; according to Jean Coussins, 93 per cent of the women beginning an apprenticeship in 1977 were intending hairdressers. On non-advanced further education courses leading to recognised qualifications, there were in 1976-77 fewer than half as many women as men. Of people aged 18 and over who had left full-time education, only 4.3 per cent of women compared with 17.7 per cent of men were on day release courses; at age 21 and over, three and one-half times as many men as women were enrolled for day release. Even in industries such as textiles — where women form a major portion of the labour force — only 753 women, but 3,649 men, were released by their employers to further education.

The most crucial area of comparison for the sexual distribution of attainment is the content of education received by girls and boys — the forms of knowledge, expertise and skill with which women and men were equipped. Whatever the academic or practical merits of particular school subjects, it would be a mistake to assume that all CSE or GCE qualifications are interchangeable; on the contrary, in terms both of career opportunities and further training, some subjects carry greater weight than others. Woodwork, metalwork and technical drawing, for example, give access to a wider range of careers, and to a greater number of technologically-based courses, than do domestic subjects. Physics and chemistry, too, have a wider currency than the biological sciences into which girls tend to be channelled. Mathematics at 'O' level or its CSE equivalent is a necessary prerequisite for careers in computer programming, textile technology, dentistry, architecture, horticulture, engineering, the police force, market research, printing, radiography, chemistry, economics, surveying, town planning, advertising, banking and astronomy — to name but a few. It is therefore of vital importance that girls as well as boys be fully represented in these subject areas.

In 1977, only 3,123 out of 137,030 'O' level and CSE candidates for technical drawing were girls, while there were 1,324 girls among the 147,854 entries for metalwork and woodwork. (At 'A' level, the sexual division was even more pronounced, with 38 girls entering for woodwork and metalwork or technical drawing, as against 4,668 boys.)

For physics and chemistry at CSE and 'O' level, there were three male candidates for every one female entry. The ratio of boys to girls entering for 'O' level mathematics was 1.4, but by 'A' level, there were 3.5 male mathematics candidates for every female candidate. For every girl who left school with two or more 'A' level passes in sciences and mathematics, there were 3.7 boys.

The differences in school attainments outlined above clearly underlie many of the stable patterns of gender differentiation in higher education. In 1976-77, only 35 per cent of undergraduates at UK universities were women. Women comprised 29 per cent of those reading for science degrees, 11 per cent of those on physics courses, 18 per cent of those studying business management, and four per cent of engineering and technology students. In polytechnics and similar colleges, 30 per cent of the students reading for CNAA first degrees, and

18 per cent of those on HND and HNC courses were women, while for technologically-based courses the discrepancies were, again, even more marked; of 70,577 full-time and part-time students on advanced courses in engineering and technology below undergraduate level, a mere 1,608 (or two per cent) were female. Women form an even smaller proportion of postgraduate students than of undergraduates — only 17 per cent of those in science subjects, for example. Even in subjects such as education, English or psychology — where women constituted 70, 60 and 62 per cent of undergraduates respectively — they formed a minority of students at postgraduate level.[1]

Do natural aptitudes explain these educational outcomes? Certain test results indicate systematic sex differences in cognitive strengths and weaknesses; for instance, in many Western societies, boys tend to lag behind girls in verbal proficiency, and girls behind boys in terms of visual-spatial perception. Such results must, however, be interpreted with extreme caution. In the first place, studies which showed no difference in performance between girls and boys have less often been submitted or accepted for publication, with the result that published data tends to exaggerate the extent of dissimilarity. Second, those sex differences which have been fairly firmly established are not great enough to account for the degree of divergence in the educational and occupational destinies of males and females. Third, research pointing to average sex differences in proficiencies generally also shows a high proportion of girls and boys whose performances overlap. Fourth, measures of proficiency reflect the different training and experience to which girls and boys are exposed, as well as any innate capacities they may possess; such measures cannot be regarded as indicating a ceiling on eventual performance of either sex. Studies have shown for example, that the spatial ability of girls can be greatly improved — and sex differences eradicated — by appropriate training programmes. All these points indicate that ostensible underlying differences in ability cannot be used to explain the outcomes of schooling which have just been documented; our concern must be with locating ways in which the schools can improve upon the weaknesses of both sexes — with ways of overcoming, rather than exacerbating, such differences as do exist. Explanations which purport to draw upon the "essential differences" between the sexes are no substitute for understanding the social construction of inequality and the points at which it can be undermined.[2]

Having documented sexual inequality, it must be added that statistics on school attainment do not tell the whole story of gender and education. While schools fail to provide girls with the qualifications necessary for (a reasonable chance of) financial independence, it is equally relevant that pupils leave school with their expectations of a conventional sexual division of labour intact. In a study of London schools reported by Tessa Blackstone and Helen Weinreich-Haste, girls of fifteen envisaged their future in terms of marriage and family commitments as well as employment, whereas boys thought only in terms of career — and a wider more challenging range of careers at that. While the ambitions and hopes of girls tend to be circumscribed by domestic obligations, many boys emerge from full-time education apparently unaware of familial and housekeeping responsibilities that should, and will, fall on their shoulders. Even amongst the university graduates whose careers were reported in *Six Years After*, almost the same proportions of men and women were married by the time the survey was conducted, but it was women and not men who had been forced to withdraw from full-time employment in order to care for the children of such marriages. The authors of the survey conclude that the persistence of the belief that women have the right to pursue careers only after their children have entered school implies "the permanent relegation of women to second-rate careers".

Now of course it must be recognised that a range of experiences outside school influence the hopes and expectations which boys and girls have of their futures. The prescriptions for happiness offered by teenage magazines and by films and television, and, more crucially, the models provided by family and friends, play an important part in this process. In attempting to explain why the performance of girls lags behind that of boys after the age of sixteen, Jenny Shaw suggests that, for girls, the prospect of marriage "discourages long-term planning"; the point of her argument is not that girls make a once-and-for-all choice between marriage and career, but rather that the conviction that marriage is inevitably just around the corner lets the girls off the hook when it comes to making decisions about their futures, and thus interferes with educational commitment at a crucial — and often irrevocable — stage. From her work with working class pupils, Sue Sharpe concludes that by the time girls see a careers advisor, their conception of "suitable" (read "available") women's employment is already firmly established. The restricted life-style of their adult acquaintances depresses their own ambitions, and orients them ever more firmly towards marriage and motherhood.

> Girls have seldom been allowed much experience outside home and school, and have read relatively little that deals comprehensively with aspects of their own lives. They see many of their relatives and friends doing jobs from which they seem to gain minimal enjoyment. It therefore makes sense to make their priorities love, marriage, husbands, children, jobs and careers, more or less in that order. . . . Their feelings and views affect areas of decision in their lives already circumscribed by factors like class and sex . . . It becomes easy for girls to acknowledge the objective worth of scholarship while excusing themselves for not being 'that sort of woman'.

Sharpe's statement highlights one of the failures of our schools: is it not remarkable that, by the fourth form of secondary school, girls have seldom been exposed to literature "that deals comprehensively with aspects of their own lives"? But her work also points to the existence of a self-perpetuating cycle, whereby the narrow range of opportunities which has been open to women, and particularly working class women, in a previous generation, weighs down the ambitions of girls in the present.

Noelle Bisseret affirms the importance of visions of past and present possibilities in shaping educational and occupational careers. She traces how class and gender enter into the ways we constitute our identities and histories. Only the dominated class and sex announce themselves as members of a particular category (I'm from a very working class background; I have a good job

14

for a woman); hence women, and all those from the dominated class, signal their awareness of themselves as different, as peripheral, as the Other. Their educational careers are more disjointed, plagued by more interruptions and false starts — the result of always having "to make some insurance for the future", of securing something to fall back on. The omniscient realities of impending marriage, family, the need to earn a living, are always pressing for recognition. Hence the educational and occupational choices of those from the dominated class and sex implicitly take account of what is (or has been) typically possible for people with their ascribed position in the social structure.

To acknowledge the existence of these influences outside the school is not, however, tantamount to saying that the school is (or must be) impotent. Rather, what it demonstrates is the intimate connections between the processes which shape the sexual distribution of achievement and those which reinforce gender differentiation. Images of what women "are", and what they might be, are integral elements in girls' decisions about their educational futures. Hence, any attempt to understand the full impact of schooling on gender divisions must analyse not only the distribution of forms of knowledge and qualifications on the basis of sex (such that women and men are channelled into separate occupational niches); it must explore also the myriad of subtle ways in which the educational process brings to life and sustains sexual divisions — the process of, quite literally, teaching girls to be women and boys to be men. During the formative years of childhood and adolescence, girls and boys spend a minimum of 15,000 hours in school. The school is, moreover, the major agency through which they are confronted in a relatively uniform way with the standards and expectations of the adult community. If this confrontation does nothing to undermine — if it perhaps even reinforces — the strong societal pressures towards a rigid sexual division of labour, we must accord a high priority to finding out how this occurs, and how it might be changed.

To grasp fully the relationship between gender and schooling, it is necessary to have a framework in which to locate the place of education in society. Although no fully satisfactory framework has yet been devised, a number of useful insights have been generated. These imply that education — far from being, as it was once ironically called, "an equality machine" — tends to act as a vehicle for the reproduction of patterns of subordination and domination which characterise our society.

In one account, schooling is said to operate within "the long shadow of work"; in other words, there is a structural similarity, or correspondence, between the organisation of production in capitalist societies, and the nature of schooling. Bowles and Gintis, the authors of this view, argue that the education system creates the conditions for the reproduction of inequality in two ways. First, schooling moulds the consciousness of pupils, investing them with the habits of thought and practice which will be required of them in their working lives; those groups, for instance, who will be expected to perform routine tasks under rigid supervision are denied opportunities in school to exercise discretion or to develop initiative. Second, though not directly creating inequality, education helps to legitimate it — to make it appear natural and acceptable. As long as most people *believe* that education operates on a meritocratic basis — as long, that is, as privilege and disadvantage are believed to result from fair competition in the educational arena, and "natural" differences in aptitude — then inequality in society appears to be justified by different levels of educational achievement. Subordinate groups are encouraged to personalise their failure; that is, to regard their disadvantage as the inevitable outcome of their own limitations — of their individual lack of intelligence, ambition or effort.

It is the contention of Bowles and Gintis that the sexual (as opposed to the social) division of labour is reproduced chiefly by means of the family; but, important as the family is, Bowles and Gintis seriously underestimate the significance of schooling. If education prepares working class pupils for subordinate positions in the class structure, so too schooling helps to shape the consciousness of pupils in such a way that girls are habituated, at every level of the educational hierarchy, to ceding priority to boys. The supposedly merito-cratic distribution of achievement serves, moreover, to legitimate and bolster sexual inequalities in economic, personal and political life.

A number of writers — particularly Ann Marie Wolpe, Rosemary Deem and Miriam David — have begun to devise theoretical accounts of education which give greater prominence to gender divisions. At the centre of their accounts is a recognition of the unique position that women occupy in the reproduction of capitalist societies. On the one hand, women in paid employment are concen-trated in that sector of the economy in which jobs are more labour intensive, less well paid and less secure. On the other, they are made responsible — by the infants they bear and rear, and the adult workers (husbands, brothers, lovers) for whom they care — for maintaining and renewing the labour force. Education helps to ensure women's continued availability for both these tasks, by producing female school leavers who are, on the whole, less well prepared to compete in the marketplace than their male counterparts, and by instilling in these girls the view that their greatest hopes of fulfilment lie in linking them-selves through home and family to a form of service that is not demanded of men.

We are reminded by these accounts that the nature of schooling does not merely reflect the demands of dominant groups or changes in the economy; on the contrary, education is "partially autonomous", the site of diverse pressures and struggles. While the theoretical emphasis is on institutions and dominant relations which condition the reproduction of inequality, recognition of the partial autonomy of education also implies that some degree of social change is possible through educational intervention — although it is clear that the struggle for a more just society must always be multi-faceted, encompassing the structure of the family, the economy and cultural forms as well as the nature of schooling. But the question of the most effective form of educational intervention depends upon an understanding of the internal workings of schools, upon knowing how curriculum, educational organisation and encounters in the classroom can be altered so as to facilitate change.

Class onto gender

While most educational research in sociology has focussed on social class, we must be cautious of transposing arguments designed to account for class inequalities on to gender. The environment — the material, social and ideological conditions which shape pupils' lives — is not the same for pupils of different sex. Two concrete examples may serve to illustrate this point. First, it is widely recognised that an important factor limiting the achievement of working class pupils is, quite simply, their families' lack of money, particularly the surplus to support children through the years between the end of compulsory schooling and the age at which they become eligible for student grants. But it may well be the case that, where families are hard-pressed financially, an extended education for daughters will be sacrificed to provide for sons; this may be part of the reason why, as several reports have shown, capable working class girls have tended to leave grammar schools earlier than their male counterparts. The material circumstances of girls and boys may differ even within the same home. Similarly, the fact that many working class girls earn pocket money through domestic duties (babysitting or housework for mothers or neighbours) while their brothers get part time jobs further afield, may be, as Angela McRobbie argues, a factor which makes the experience and the horizons of working class girls more circumscribed than that of their brothers.

Nor do schools necessarily provide the same "environment" for girls and boys of similar socio-economic backgrounds. Independent schools, for example, draw most of their pupils from privileged social backgrounds, and confer on them certain educational and social advantages. However, while boys from independent schools go on to secure a disproportionate share of elite positions in the civil service, the judiciary, and the top ranks of industry, the future of their female contemporaries is very different. Girls at fee-paying schools are less likely to be prepared for leadership, and more likely, as Judith Okely puts it, to "learn to live ambitions only vicariously", through the influential men they are groomed to attract and marry.

Both these examples illustrate that boys and girls — even in similar family, social class, or school — inhabit, to some extent, separate social worlds. Elaboration of these worlds, of their differences and interconnections becomes more urgent given the gradual replacement of single-sex selective schools by mixed sex comprehensives. It was remarked by Westergaard and Resler that one of the unintended consequences of comprehensive re-organisation — which was partially designed to reduce inequality between social classes — was to disguise that inequality by rendering it invisible within the same school. A similar process may take place with the merging of single-sex schools. The fact that girls and boys are gathered together under the same roof should not blind us to the many ways in which the experience of schooling may disadvantage members of one sex or the other. Only recently have certain aspects of coeducational schooling which may sabotage hopes of gender equality — the structuring of pupil choice, the nature of the curriculum, and the link between teachers' expectations and classroom interaction — begun to attract the attention they deserve.

sexist attitudes

Choice

Apart from any formal curricular differences imposed on girls and boys by schools and colleges — some of which may be challenged under the Sex Discrimination Act — marked divergences in expertise arise through the choices pupils make with respect to subject options and careers. Whether we look at CSE, 'O' level or 'A' level examination entries, at further education courses or university enrolments, the same pattern obtains: women are clustered in arts, languages and social science fields; they are far less likely than men to pursue scientific, mathematical and technical subjects. This pattern is more marked in co-educational schools, where despite a generally wider range of options, pupils' choices tend to be more sex-stereotyped than in single-sex establishments.

Subject

Subject choices at secondary school have, as we have seen, important ramifications for the kinds of employment and training which are open to girls and boys in later life. Eileen Byrne's proposal of a core curriculum for every girl and boy up to the age of 16, a curriculum consisting not only of science and maths, English and languages, but also preparation for parenthood, may be the most practical long-term solution for ensuring that all young people leave school with adequate grounding for later life. But in the absence of such a policy, we must be alert to the ways in which the choices of girls and boys, particularly at the secondary level, are channelled by the school.

Timetable

Extreme specialisation along gender lines is encouraged, firstly, by certain timetabling practices. The 1975 report by Her Majesty's Inspectorate on curricular differentiation found, for example, that over a quarter of schools blocked subjects on the timetable in such a way that it was difficult for an arts-inclined pupil to "dabble" in sciences, or for a scientifically-oriented pupil to pursue certain arts subjects. A further quarter of schools had pre-emptive patterns of curriculum choice, some of which would clearly reduce the opportunities for girls or boys to experiment with "deviant" subjects; one such case was the offering of technical drawing on an optional basis to all pupils, while accepting only those who had previously studied metalwork (from which girls were excluded).

There are, however, other more routine ways in which an apparently free choice may be socially constrained. An open choice is not necessarily an easy one to make; it takes considerably more determination (and support) for a boy or girl to choose a subject or career which is not considered appropriate to their gender. This is even more likely to be the case in mixed schools where, as Jenny Shaw suggests, pupils may be anxious to highlight the boundaries between themselves and the other sex. Teachers or careers advisors can easily assume a decisive role in the process of pupil choice. A neutral stance on a teacher's part — a reluctance to speak whole-heartedly in favour of the non-traditional option — would be enough to tip the balance in favour of the more conventional choice. But can we assume that teachers are neutral in this respect? On the contrary, what little evidence there is available suggests that teachers and careers advisors may wittingly or unwittingly steer girls and boys towards traditionally feminine

18

or masculine goals. In my own research, for example, some teachers reported
that they found it difficult to take seriously girls' ambitions, especially when a
pupil had a traditionally feminine demeanour.

> Susan is really rather hard and determined, but she's blonde. I've got
> nothing against that, poor girl, but she's got the superficial characteristic of
> being a rather dizzy blonde, and yet underneath it she's got this hard streak
> of wanting to get on. I can't reconcile the two.

Statements such as this suggest that there may be a need for teachers to monitor
carefully the verbal advice they give to their pupils. Under the Sex Discrimination Act, careers literature must be scanned to eliminate blatantly sexist
material; a booklet on business careers, for example, which portrayed men as
executives and women as typists would be illegal. Unfortunately, the sexist
assumptions which may underlie teachers' part in the selection process are
harder to root out.

But even the most sincere and energetic efforts to get boys and girls to re-
think their choices of subject and career, to broaden their horizons beyond the
traditional bounds of gender, will be thwarted to the extent that schools
continue, in other areas of practice, to re-create gender divisions. For example,
the customary division of labour in many schools — with girls encouraged to
look after visitors, comfort younger pupils, and make tea for the visitors and
parents while boys are expected to move the chairs for a meeting in the hall —
does nothing to undermine stereotypical views of the competences and weaknesses of one sex or the other. The wisdom of regulations which allow the
wearing of trousers only for male pupils can be questioned; anyone who has had
the experience of wearing both skirts and trousers will recognise the truth of the
claim that the special uniforms required for girls can often be more restrictive
and more inhibiting than those of boys. The games encouraged for girls — net-
ball, hockey — not only carry less prestige than soccer, rugby or cricket, but are
less readily pursued into adult life. A host of practices which may on the surface
seem trivial — from the habit of addressing girls and only girls by their first
names, to the teasing remarks which teachers sometimes direct at their female
pupils — may transmit messages concerning the appropriateness of gender as a
differentiating principle, and contribute to the conceptions pupils hold of
masculinity and femininity. The point I wish to make is a simple one: the
factors that inhibit more adventurous choices are not confined to the moment of
decision-making. Schools cannot replicate the sexist nature of the world outside
and still expect to be taken seriously when, in a careers talk, they say to girls,
"The world is your oyster".

Curriculum

Apart from the fact that different subjects are sometimes provided for girls and
boys, the teaching of the same subjects to girls and boys in mixed schools can,
nevertheless, have the effect of reproducing gender divisions. At the most
obvious level, this may happen when pupils are split into groups on the basis of

sex. The 1975 report on curricular differentiation noted that 98 per cent of coeducational schools segregate girls and boys for some aspects of their work; this was usually justified by headteachers not on educational grounds, but for reasons of organisational convenience.

The convenience of sex-segregation may be outweighed by its disadvantageous side-effects — the reinforcement, for example, of taken-for-granted views of "innate" gender differences in interests or abilities. As Jenny Shaw remarked, the treatment of sex as an appropriate basis for educational organisation does "nothing to counteract the marked tendency towards role segregation based on sex in the home and elsewhere". Sex segregation in schools may, moreover, reduce the opportunities pupils have to test gender stereotypes against the actual behaviour of classmates of the other sex; it is interesting that the subjects shown in Benn and Simon's survey of mixed comprehensives to be frequently prohibited to one sex or the other, were precisely those subjects (pottery, dancing, gardening, catering, woodwork, infant care, and building) that are most likely to involve relaxed interaction and collective effort on the part of pupils. Finally, the significance of sex segregation in schools may be greater than its frequency in the timetable might suggest; the few situations in which girls and boys are treated differently may assume a particular importance with respect to evolving definitions of femininity and masculinity.

Where girls and boys are taught in mixed classes, the style of teaching may yet incline pupils to believe that the subject is more appropriate for one sex than the other. This has been found to happen, for instance, with the teaching of woodwork or housecraft to mixed classes; teachers sometimes impress upon girls the absolute necessity of learning efficient ways of shopping, cooking or mending clothing, while encouraging boys to "have a go" on the understanding that they may occasionally have to perform simple household duties if their wife is ill. Sometimes the shoe is on the other foot; boys in woodwork classes are required to produce competent pieces of work, while the female pupils are treated as dilettantes. It is hardly surprising that pupils may emerge from such shared classes with a heightened conviction that domestic tasks are the property of women, and woodwork the province of men.

The teaching of sciences may provide yet another example. Many science textbooks have been written, apparently, with a male readership in mind; this comes across in the illustrations in which boys are more likely to be the ones who hold the test tube or adjust the bunsen burner.[3] Research such as Alison Kelly's suggests that both boys and girls do come to share the view that certain branches of science — chemistry, physics, electronics — are more suitable for men than for women. In addition, Wolpe argues that the examples that are used by teachers in an effort to make subjects relevant to everyday life, all too often relate mathematical as well as scientific technique to activities — such as map-reading, calculation of crop yields and aeronautics — with which boys can more readily identify than girls.

The sociology of education points, however, to a much more fundamental series of questions concerning the curriculum. The view that schools transmit our common cultural heritage has given way, in recent years, to a recognition that out of the enormous range of ideas, values and knowledge available in any culture, only a fraction is selected as suitable for transmission in schools. The question then becomes: what are the criteria behind this selection, and which social groups benefit from the exclusion of competing forms of thought? Bernstein, and Bourdieu and Passeron, for example, have in their different ways attempted to show that the intellectual styles espoused by schools, and the forms of expression which are valued and rewarded, correspond more closely to dominant groups' experience of the world than to others'.

Nowhere is an understanding of the conditions governing the emergence of a partial curriculum, and of its effects, more urgent than in the area of gender divisions. Feminist analyses of literature, of art, of history, of the social sciences, of medicine and so on have revealed the remarkable extent to which those disciplines incorporate untenable sexist assumptions and biases — for example, the extent to which the writing of working class history has been confined to the activities of working class men. The teaching of subjects such as these at secondary level understandably reflects these biases; social studies, literature and history syllabuses in particular fail to give full due to the range of activity of both sexes, and incorporate values and assumptions which downgrade and devalue women's experience and achievement.

It is clearly not teachers who are at fault here, but the patriarchal structure of knowledge itself, which tends to omit women, on the one hand, and to particularise their experience on the other. Teachers may, however, feel threatened by such critiques, both because they appear to weaken notions of academic objectivity (and thereby indirectly undermine one of a teacher's sources of authority), and because teachers may see the re-appraisal of their subject in the light of such critiques as a challenge to their own professional integrity and identity. The solution lies, it seems to me, in recognising the exciting academic and pedagogical challenge posed by these critiques. We are presented with a unique opportunity to consider the ways in which particular subjects may have been subtly (or not so subtly) distorted by patriarchal assumptions; an opportunity to explore the distance between our own lives and that portrayed in the literature; and, finally, an opportunity to stimulate pupils to ask new and more searching questions of the material they study.

It is impossible to conclude a discussion of the curriculum without dealing with language, the very medium in which teaching and learning proceeds. Language provides perhaps the clearest example of how, at the deepest but least intentional level, our teaching often conveys to pupils the sense that men, and only men, are the initiators, the active agents, the subjects of human life. When we say, "American colonists took their wives and children to the New World" — instead of "American colonist families travelled to the New World" — what are we teaching pupils about the passivity of women and children, or about the impossibility of women taking action except under the protection of a man? By such everyday statements as "inventors and their wives", or "a scientist must devote his every waking hour", or "primitive man discovered fire", we fail to name women and thereby exclude them from vast areas of human culture and experience. Where we name women and only women (as in the statement "a woman athlete" or "a woman physicist") we convey the impression that athletes, or physicists, are normally, typically, (properly?) male.

For those who continue to believe that words like "mankind" or "he" are generic terms which everyone knows embrace females as well as males, it is worth pointing out that research with pupils from primary schools upwards has shown this not to be the case. Under experimental conditions, for example, children illustrate stories about primitive "man" with drawings of men to whom they give unambiguously male names. Even among university students — who are surely more aware of linguistic conventions — the word "man" is usually taken to refer to adult males. This was demonstrated by a study in which American college students were asked to select appropriate illustrations for a forthcoming sociology textbook. Those who were given chapter headings such as "Social Man", "Industrial Man" and "Political Man", overwhelmingly produced pictures of adult males engaged in social, industrial and political activity. Other students, whose chapter titles included "Society", "Industrial Life" and "Political Behaviour", selected a far higher proportion of illustrations showing girls as well as boys, women as well as men. If phrases such as "the ascent of man" have the effect, as Miller and Swift conclude, of "filtering out the recognition of women's participation in these major areas of life", the significance for gender divisions of the way we employ language in our everyday teaching should be clear.[4]

Teachers' expectations and classroom interaction

Differential reactions to women and men are a taken for granted pa[rt of everyday] day life. Parents may scarcely be aware that they praise their daughters [for being] pretty and loving, their sons for being courageous and resourceful. Behaviour which is applauded in a woman ("she is sweet and gentle") may be condemned in a man ("he is effeminate"). Of course, the reverse may also be true: a male executive may be admired for being "forceful" and "determined", while his female counterpart is accused of being "pushy" and "stubborn".

May have been dismissed because typical male behaviour?

We need to develop a greater understanding of the way teachers' notions of masculinity and femininity shape their relationships with boys and with girls, and of the effects these have on their pupils. Research in the USA suggests that pre-school and primary teachers believe their pupils to conform closely to gender stereotypes (boys active, aggressive and extroverted; girls passive, dependent and introverted) even when attempts at objective measurement show no such clear-cut differences between boys and girls. It seems likely that where teachers hold such expectations about the interests, abilities, conduct and personality of their male and female pupils that they may, by the encouragement they give and the stimuli they provide, heighten any such differences as may exist, and create special problems for the girl or the boy who does not conform to type.

It is important to emphasise that differential expectations of girls and boys need not be synonymous with prejudice or discrimination in any straightforward sense. Nell Keddie's study "Classroom Knowledge" recognised a disparity of attitudes between the "educationist context" (where teachers theorise about the aims and nature of learning) and the teaching context (where they are forced to cope with the complex demands of the classroom). We should not be surprised then, when teachers who are strongly committed to equality of the sexes, nevertheless regard boys as more enthusiastic, more logical and more able to grasp new concepts — as was true of teachers of fifth form pupils in the urban comprehensives studied by Lynn Davies. Davies and Meighan comment that "Girls' complaints about receiving less attention in class may well be justified if teachers do reveal their appreciation of the boys' dynamic personality characteristics".

Moreover, those aspects of classroom interaction which contribute most forcefully to reinforcing gender divisions may often be (from the teacher's point of view) incidental to the real business of teaching. For example, in the sixth form department where my research was conducted, male teachers often interspersed their lectures with good-natured jokes of a mildly flirtatious sort. "Good heavens, Jane, I didn't realise you had legs!" (addressed to a pupil who appears for the first time that year in a skirt) is a typical remark: while jokes about role reversal, humorous appeals to "we men v. you girls", and mild sexual innuendoes are used to promote a "friendly" atmosphere in the classroom. Although their relationships with pupils are shot through with considerations of sexuality, as well as of the sexual division of labour, these teachers declare — and there is no reason to doubt their sincerity — that "when it comes down to business" they are, in their dealings with girls and boys, scrupulously fair. The important point is not that girls are being "discriminated against", in the sense of being graded more harshly or denied educational opportunities: but that the classroom is a venue in which girls and boys, dependent upon a man (or woman) who has a considerable degree of power over their immediate comfort and long-term future, can hardly avoid becoming enmeshed in a process whereby "normal" relationships between the sexes are being constantly defined.

The links between teachers' expectations and patterns of classroom interaction are still imperfectly understood. A number of surveys have indicated that the majority of teachers in secondary schools, both male and female, prefer to work with boys. Moreover, studies which have involved protracted observation of a variety of classrooms have shown, almost invariably, that boys receive a disproportionate share of teachers' time and attention. High achieving boys are in some studies a particularly favoured group, claiming more of their teachers' energies than either similarly performing girls, or than less successful pupils of either sex. On the other hand, although girls are criticised at least as often as boys for academic mistakes, boys are far more often reprimanded for misconduct — and, in some classrooms, these criticisms account for a large share of the extra attention directed at boys.

But these data tell only part of the story. For one thing, we do not know whether teachers' preference for their male pupils, as revealed in interviews, is reflected in the *quality* of relationships that teachers establish with boys and girls, for quality is not readily susceptible to measurement. For another, concentration on the spoken exchanges between teachers and pupils may overlook some of the less visible but equally important elements of classroom life; Carol Dweck reports that teachers may reinforce the stereotypica' ^' boys and girls as much by the kinds of actions they overloo directly commented upon. Finally, we need to develop a sys ing of how girls and boys themselves interpret classroom enc their experience of classroom life influences their views about the worth and capabilities of the sexes. For example, by more frequently criticising their male pupils, teachers may unwittingly reinforce the idea that the 'naughtiness' of boys is more interesting, more deserving of attention, than the 'niceness' of girls.

The research[5]

What follows is an attempt to explore these issues further — to shed some light on the practices of pupils and especially of teachers which actively reproduce a hierarchical system of gender divisions in and through the classroom. The research draws upon detailed individual interviews with teachers, and with a sample of their male and female pupils, in seven 'A' level classes. The objective was not to produce a description of events in the classroom as they might appear to an impartial observer, but rather to capture the quality of classroom life as currently experienced by pupils themselves. How, I wished to know, do girls and boys make sense of their educational experience? What effect does this have for their own self-image, and for their views of their own and the other sex? The design of the sample and the structure of the interviews made it possible to trace connections or inconsistencies between, on the one hand, teachers' attitudes towards pupils of either sex, and, on the other, the character of classroom life as reported by the pupils themselves.

A brief word about the background to the research may be helpful. I chose to focus on 'A' level classes in the humanities department of a college of further education with a large sixth form intake partly because of the absence, in this setting, of more obvious forms of gender differentiation: in this department, all classes are coeducational; academic and extracurricular activities are technically open to all pupils, male or female; type of dress can be freely chosen; there are relatively few regulations concerning conduct, and certainly none to my knowledge that differentiate between girls and boys; the proportions of female pupils and female staff are much higher than in, say, the maths and science department; and the girls are, in terms of academic performance, as successful as the boys. In short, one would expect that if any mixed educational establishment would avoid the marginalisation of girls — the definition of female pupils as "second-rate citizens" — it might happen in a relatively liberal setting such as this. As the research proceeded, however, it became apparent that fairly subtle aspects of classroom encounters continued to regenerate a sexual hierarchy of worth, in which men emerged as the "naturally" dominant sex. Whether a similar dynamic operates amongst, say, pupils aged 12 or 13 in the lower streams of comprehensive schools remains to be seen.[6]

Looked at stereotypical -
Patriarchal views of teachers
towards their pupils.
- Gen categorizing nurses &
shop. teaching type jobs to
girls - civil service & managerial
type jobs to boys -
- even when obviously less
intelligent. - Also looked at preconceptions pupils held about their
teachers - men for example being
seen as better disciplinarians

PART II

GIRLS ON THE MARGINS:
A STUDY OF GENDER DIVISIONS IN THE CLASSROOM

A. The significance of gender in teachers' views of their pupils

Teacher: As I told his father, he's not really got any friends in our group. Because he's not like Norman, who's the acting one, and he's not like Sebastian who's the public school type. He is just a nice quiet ordinary sort of lad. In the back row, I'm afraid, the boys have got their own groups of friends. One of them is a rugger player, and the other two stick pretty closely together. He doesn't seem to fit. And the rest are girls.

How important a factor is gender in teachers' perceptions of their pupils? The obstacles confronting systematic research into teachers' orientations towards male and female pupils are formidable. Differential perceptions of boys and girls may be so taken for granted by teachers that they will rarely, and only with great difficulty, be explicitly articulated. Furthermore, differential attitudes towards *particular* groups of girls and boys may co-exist with egalitarian principles which inhibit their expression anywhere but in the classroom itself; as Nell Keddie demonstrated in her study "Classroom Knowledge", there may be a gulf between the ideals teachers profess in the abstract, and the prejudices they enact in the classroom. With these difficulties in mind, teachers were not asked direct questions about their attitudes to gender. Instead, the interviews concentrated on their attitudes towards, and perceptions of, the particular pupils whom they regularly teach; and did so in such a way that attitudes to male and female pupils can be systematically analysed, and can be compared with the comments of the pupils themselves.

Segregation in co-educational classes?

Teachers carry in their heads an impressive range of information about individual pupils for whom they are responsible; this is true at least of the teachers I know, and certainly of the teachers interviewed in this study. But is it the case that the male/female distinction acts as a fundamental anchor point for the way teachers categorise their pupils?

A special procedure was used to investigate the possibility that teachers would be more sensitive to similarities between pupils of the same sex, than to characteristics which girls and boys may have in common. Each teacher was presented with a number of co-ed triads (a set of cards bearing the names of two boys and one girl, or two girls and one boy) and invited to pair the two pupils who were, in some educationally relevant way, most alike. A calculation was made of the number of occasions on which teachers paired the two pupils of the same sex. Overall, there was only a moderate tendency for teachers to confine their comparisons to pupils of the same sex. There were, however, marked differences between the choices made by female teachers and those made by men. Of the co-ed triads considered by female teachers, only 39 per cent were sorted into same-sex pairs. Male teachers, by contrast, selected same-sex pairs in 80 per cent of the cases.

There might be several ways of explaining this finding. First, it might be suggested that male teachers consider gender itself to be evidence of, or explanation for, different educational skills. Such attitudes are not unknown among the teachers interviewed, as the following comment suggests; the remark is, however, atypical of teachers' statements, and was made by a woman rather than a man.

> *Female teacher:* On the other hand, Nick, being a boy, he's rather slapdash. The girls write more diligent essays.

Another explanation for same-sex pairings might be that, perhaps because of different upbringings, girls are more likely to resemble their female classmates than their male ones, in ways that are significant within an educational context; and that, therefore, the pairing of girls with girls, and boys with boys, merely reflects teachers' perceptions of the "actual" characteristics of their pupils. This suggestion must be rejected, because it cannot account for the different patterns of choice between male and female teachers. If girls are radically different from boys in the classroom, how is it that male teachers paired pupils of the same sex twice as frequently as female teachers?

The most adequate explanation of the findings is that male teachers tend, far more than their female colleagues, to view the sexes whom they teach in mixed classes as relatively discrete groups. If male teachers are particularly attuned to dissimilarity between the sexes, this orientation may, in turn, be translated into actions which have the effect of further polarising girls and boys in classes which they teach. (As we shall see later on, this possibility is borne out by pupils' comments.) In sum, the pairings made by male teachers may reflect both their own way of looking at the world (through a framework which emphasises male/ female dissimilarity), and behavioural differences between girls and boys which the men's own attitudes may help to create.

Attachment, concern and rejection

Teachers were asked a series of questions to elicit the names of pupils to whom they were most attached, for whom they were most concerned, and those whom they would most readily reject. In analysing the responses, an effort was made to control for pupils' academic standing: whether, that is, pupils are classified by teachers as likely to pass, on the borderline, or likely to fail. Even when academic standing is taken into account, it is clear that gender plays a large part in the character of teachers' involvements with their pupils.

Teachers are most often attached to, and concerned for, pupils who are expected to pass. Within this group, however, boys are twice as likely as girls to receive "concern" from their teachers, and three times as likely to receive "attachment" choices. In addition, the only pupils among those classified as borderline or fail for whom teachers showed concern, were boys.

"Rejection" was most often directed at pupils who were in danger of failing their examinations. But a girl in this category is twice as likely to be rejected as a boy of the same standing. Furthermore, the only pupils from the pass category to be rejected were girls.

The evidence that teachers are more attached to and concerned for boys, and more often reject girls, applies to teachers of both sexes. However, the trend is more pronounced among the male teachers; the chance, for example, that a boy will be the recipient of his teacher's concern is twice that of a girl if the teacher is a woman, but ten times greater if the teacher is a man.

Initial impressions of pupils: "Just three quiet girls"

In the early weeks of the academic year, teachers are faced with the arduous task of getting to know not just one, but several, groups of pupils; it is not surprising that it takes a while for the name and face of every pupil to be clearly linked in teachers' minds. What is remarkable is that the pupils who were mentioned by teachers as being difficult to place were, without exception, girls.

Interviewer: What were your first impressions of Emma?
Male teacher: Nothing really. I can only remember first impressions of a few who stood out right away; Adrian of course; and Philip; and David Levick; and Marion, too, because among the girls she was the earliest to say something in class. In fact, it was quite a time before I could tell some of the girls apart.
Interviewer: Who was that?
Teacher: Well, Angie, and her friends Leonore and Helen. They seemed rather silent at first, and they were friends, I think, and there was no way — that's how it seemed at the time — of telling one from the other. In fact, they are very different in appearance, I can see that now. One's fair and one's dark, for a start. But at the beginning they were just three quiet girls.

Interviewer: What were your first impressions of Lucy?
Female teacher: I didn't start teaching that class until a bit later, by which time my mind was dulled. Although I had seen them once a week, she hadn't made any impression on me at all. I didn't know which one she was. She was one of the people who it took me longest to cotton on to her name. She was one I got mixed up, actually, with Sharon, who was equally quiet and somewhat the same build. Now they're quite different, I realise, but at the time I was never quite sure which one it was.
Interviewer: So Lucy was very slow to make any impression at all then?
Teacher: Well, a positive impression, yes. I won't say she made a negative impression, but . . . well, you see the trouble is that that group had got more girls in it, which makes a difference. The other group had a lot of foreigners, and within a day or two I knew Belinda, who was the only foreign girl. And Dennis had curly hair and Tony had straight hair, so they were well fixed in. In fact, in that group there were only Lyn and Judith

who took me a few days to get straightened out, and the rest I knew
straight away. Whereas in this group, there were only seven boys and about
ten girls, I suppose.
Interviewer: So you found it easiest to learn the names of the boys, did you?
Teacher: Yes, that's it.

As these quotations suggest, the anonymity of girls is due in part to their
reticence. The girl who is mentioned as speaking out early is instantly "fixed" by
her teacher; she has, among the girls, a sort of rarity value. However, this cannot
entirely explain the greater readiness with which teachers identify boys, for the
few male pupils who were reported by their teachers to be exceptionally quiet in
class were, nevertheless, clearly remembered. Teachers' slowness at identifying
girls has strong implications for the comfort and involvement of female pupils
for, as we shall see later on, pupils take it as a sign of approval if teachers know
their names right away.

Advice and expectation

Teachers were asked what advice they would give to particular pupils if they
were considering abandoning 'A' levels either in order to get married, or to take
a job. Many of the teachers refused to accept that marriage might imply an
interruption of studies; as one woman exclaimed (perhaps drawing on her own
experience in combining marriage and academic work), "I don't know why you
think marriage is such a disruptive activity!" For the rest of the teachers, the
advice offered was often cautionary, and female pupils were warned against
giving up 'A' levels as often as males — although, as the first passage below
indicates, some men were worried that to advise a girl against early marriage
might be taken as a slur on her character.

> *Male teacher:* Don't do it. I would say, "Don't do it." Don't get me wrong,
> she could certainly cope with marriage, she wouldn't be an inept house-
> keeper or a child-beater or anything like that. But if she could get her
> qualifications before she took all that on, I'd say stay.
> *Male teacher:* If Sheila's getting married meant giving up her chance of
> getting 'A' levels, I'd say it would be disastrous.
> *Male teacher:* I'd probably tell Howard the story of my life, how easy it was
> to get married and how difficult it was to get back. I would remind him of
> the disadvantages.
> *Female teacher:* I think I'd say that nowadays, in her age group, half the
> marriages will end in divorce by the time they're thirty. And although she
> may have got a boyfriend whom she feels she's going to love for life, you
> don't know what's going to happen. I've told some of them in the past,
> that your husband may die (because accidents do happen!) and you'll have
> to support the family, and if you don't have two 'A' levels it is much
> harder to start again.

Largely because of the steadier academic record of their female pupils,
teachers were less likely to dissuade boys than girls from giving up 'A' levels to
take a job; only one teacher made the point that it might be more risky for girls
in general to abandon their studies than for boys:

Female teacher: I think I would say no . . . The type of jobs girls get offered are rather different from the ones boys get offered. It's likely to be a job lacking in prospects; and it's also quite a lot harder for girls to come back to academic study than it is for men.

The most important point to emerge from this section of the interviews is that teachers tended to find the questions much less credible for their male pupils than for their female ones. When asked about their male pupils, teachers commented that it was very unlikely the boy would contemplate leaving college for employment (in one-third of the cases) or for marriage (in one-half).

Male teacher: To take a job? Now? I don't think that's even conceivable. It's like having Alastair McMaster (a teacher noted for being very untrendy) announce he was off to join a rock group.
Female teacher: I'd be amazed. I can't imagine Ted thinking of marriage. He's definitely still got the schoolboy atmosphere. I don't think he'd have the kind of maturity to cope with a girl at this stage.
Male teacher: Well, it wouldn't arise, would it? Boys don't usually give up their studies when they get married, that's what girls are more inclined to do.

No equivalent comments were passed about girls. It appears that while teachers are equally concerned that girls and boys should avoid a disruption of study due to marriage, and more concerned to prevent the girls abandoning their studies for employment, teachers *expect* such disruptions more often from girls than from boys. In other words, teachers feel at least as strongly that girls should complete their 'A' levels compared with boys; but they combine this with a lower expectation that girls will actually do so.

Looking to the future

Teachers were asked to predict what each of their pupils might be doing two years, and five years, from the time of the interview. Boys — even those in danger of failing their examinations — were seen in jobs involving considerable responsibility and authority, the most frequent predictions being for civil service or management careers. One boy, for example, of whom his teacher had earlier said — "His essays are bald, childlike and undeveloped; his statements are simple and naive" — was expected to rise to head office:

Female teacher: I suspect he might be quite good at summing things up. I don't know quite whether local government or civil service, but I can't just see him pushing paper around. I can see him writing reports on things. Perhaps an information officer, or sales planning, or something like that; something in head office.

Marriage cropped up in teachers' predictions of boys' future only once, in the case of a pupil who was academically very weak, but in whom his teachers recognised exceptional personal qualities; they described him as having "a warm streak, almost Mediterranean", and "the gift of communication" (a reference to his sympathetic manner in face-to-face encounters, for he was reported not to speak in class). He alone among the boys is defined more in terms of his personality than his ability, and it may be no accident that he is the *only* boy for whom the future anticipated by his teachers includes marriage and parenthood.

> *Male teacher:* I wonder if he's the kind of boy who will marry fairly young, once he's sure of his sexual self as it were.
> *Female teacher:* I see him having a frightfully happy girlfriend who's terribly fond of him. So long as she's not ambitious, I think they'll be very happy. He would be a super father. I think children would adore having him for a father, though I'm not immediately sure what he'd be doing to support his family.

By contrast, the occupations suggested for girls seldom ranged beyond the stereotype of secretary, nurse or teacher. These predictions do not match either the girls' academic standing or their own aspirations. For instance, the girl who is envisaged as a secretary in the following quotation is thought to be fully capable of getting a university degree, and is herself considering a career in law.

> *Female teacher:* I can imagine her being a very competent, if somewhat detached, secretary. She looks neat and tidy, her work's neat and tidy, she's perfectly prompt at arriving. And she moves around with an air of knowing what she's doing. She doesn't drift.
> *Interviewer:* Why would she be a *detached* secretary?
> *Teacher:* I can't imagine her falling for her boss at all! or getting in a flap.
> *Interviewer:* What about in five years' time?
> *Teacher:* Well, I can see her having a family, and having them jolly well organised. They'll get up at the right time and go to school at the right time, wearing the right clothes. Meals will be ready when her husband gets home. She'll handle it jolly well.

Another girl, who intends to qualify as a professional psychologist, is predicted, in five years' time, to be at home with the children:

> *Female teacher:* I don't know what she's got in mind, but I can imagine her being a nurse. She's got a very responsible attitude to life. I don't know if nursing would be the best thing for her, but something like that, something which is demanding.
> *Interviewer:* What about being a doctor, say?
> *Teacher:* I don't think she has quite enough academic capacity for that, but she might go into teaching. A caring kind of vocation, that's what I see her in.
> *Interviewer:* What about in five years' time?
> *Teacher:* Obviously married. She's the sort of girl who could very easily be married in five years' time.
> *Interviewer:* Would she be working then. do you think?
> *Teacher:* She might. But she's the sort of girl, I think, to stay at home with the children. She's a caring person, as I said.

Remarks such as this indicate an implicit assumption that girls' capacities for efficiency and initiative will be channelled into nurturant or subordinate occupations (and, of course, into childcare and housework) rather than into other, less traditional, spheres.

Marriage and parenthood figure prominently in teachers' visions of the futures of their *female* pupils: teachers volunteered that two-thirds of the girls would be married in the near future. The prediction of marriage was applied not only to girls whose academic record was unremarkable, as here —

> *Male teacher:* She is the sort of girl who might up and get married all of a
> sudden, and kick over the traces.
> *Interviewer:* You mean she might abandon her 'A' levels?
> *Teacher:* I'm not saying she would, but I wouldn't be surprised.
> *Interviewer:* What do you imagine her doing in five years' time?
> *Teacher:* Definitely married.

— but also to girls who were considered to have outstanding academic capacity.

> *Male teacher:* Well, I'd be surprised if she wasn't married.
> *Interviewer:* Is she the sort of person you would expect to marry young?
> *Teacher:* Well, not necessarily marry young, but let's see . . . 16, 17, 18, 19
> years old . . . somewhere along the line, certainly. I can't see what she'd be
> doing apart from that.

In only one instance when teachers anticipated the future was the possibility of early marriage viewed regretfully, as a potential interruption to a girl's development:

> *Male teacher:* I should like to see her doing some kind of higher education,
> and I wonder whether something in the HND line might be more suitable
> than a degree course.
> *Interviewer:* Because it's slightly more practical?
> *Teacher:* Yes. This is pure supposition, but it does seem to me that there is a
> practical vein in her. She successfully holds down a job in one of the chain
> stores. I can see her making a very great success of management, retail
> management, because I would have thought she would be very skilled at
> dealing with people. And though she's a little unsure of herself still, there
> is a vein of sureness in her. She wouldn't be taken aback by awkward
> situations, for instance.
> *Interviewer:* What about in five years' time?
> *Teacher:* Quite possibly early marriage, which I think would be a pity. Not
> because I'm against the institution of marriage, but because I think that an
> early marriage would prevent her from fully realising her potential.

Apart from the reaction to marriage, the preceding quotation is a-typical of teachers' comments about their female pupils in other respects. First, it is the only prediction in which a management post was suggested for a girl. Second, the fact that a possible career was specified by a male teacher is itself unusual; in two-thirds of male teachers' discussions of female pupils, the girl could not be envisaged in any occupation once her education was complete. In some cases, it is almost as if the working lives of women are a mystery to men:

Male teacher: She would be competent enough to do a course at a university or polytechnic, though not necessarily the most academic course.
Interviewer: What sort of a course might suit her then?
Teacher: I can't say. I don't really know about jobs for girls.

Male teacher: She will probably go on to further or higher education. You'd know better than I what a young girl with an independent sort of mind might be doing in five years' time!

The type of futures teachers anticipate for girls seem to be related to class-room interaction in two important ways. First, teachers' views of "women's work", and their emphasis upon the centrality of family in women's lives, are likely to make high achievement at 'A' level seem less urgent for girls than for boys. To the extent that teachers underestimate the ambitions of their female pupils, they will be reluctant to make girls prime candidates for attention in the classroom. Second — and more pertinent to this study — it seems likely that the current dynamic of classroom interaction does nothing to undermine stereo-typical views of appropriate spheres for women and men. The reports gathered here from both teachers and pupils indicate that (whatever girls may be like outside) they are in the classroom quieter, more diffident and less openly com-petitive than their male classmates. No matter how conscientious and capable female pupils are, they are perceived by their teachers to lack the authoritative manner and the assertiveness which many teachers seem to believe to be pre-requisites of "masculine" occupations.

This interpretation seems to be the best way of accounting for a curious anomaly in the teachers' predictions. One girl who is ranked as the top performer in both her main subjects, and who wants a career in the diplomatic service, is envisaged by her teacher as the "personal assistant to somebody rather impor-tant". In contrast, the girl with the poorest academic record is one of only two girls to be suggested for a job that is not in the traditional feminine mould. The comments made about these two pupils are reproduced below; they indicate that teachers attach a great significance to assertiveness in classroom situations.

Interviewer: And can you think ahead to five years' time, what Clare might be doing in five years' time?
Female teacher: I could possibly see her as a kind of committee type person. She's not a forceful public speaker, you see. She says something rather quietly, and it's absolutely right. The people next to her take it in, but it doesn't have any impact if you see what I mean. I can imagine her as the personal assistant to somebody rather important, dealing with things very competently, and arranging things very competently, and giving ideas backwards and forwards, and dealing with individual callers face to face. She's good at face to face things, or in small groups, rather than in large groups.
Interviewer: What about Alison in five years' time?
Female teacher: She could have a professional job of some sort, I think. I can imagine her in publicity or almost anything. She's got a strong presence, and she definitely makes an impression. She's pretty downright and forthright and forthcoming in her opinions. In fact, she is a very good stimulus in the group, though she does make some of the pupils feel a bit antagonistic.

It is, apparently, only when a girl's behaviour in class sharply contradicts the retiring feminine stereotype (a contradiction that may produce antagonism from classmates), that teachers are likely to imagine her in a career at odds with highly traditional expectations.

B. Pupils' interpretation of teachers

Interviewer: When you think of a successful historian, what sort of image comes to mind?
Female pupil: Actually, I usually think of men as being historians.
Interviewer: Why's that, do you think?
Pupil: I don't know. It's like I always think of women doing English.
Interviewer: Is it because your history teachers were always men before?
Pupil: No, they have always been women, actually . . . I never thought of my history teachers as being *historians* at all.
Interviewer: What did you think they were?
Pupil: Just ordinary middle-aged women.

Preconceptions about gender: authority and discipline

Although pupils were not questioned about discipline in the classroom, many ventured criticisms of teachers for being, in their view, insufficiently authoritarian.

Male pupil: He's too nervous, I think, to put them down. They could be joking, they could be laughing, they could be doing anything and he would just pretend nothing was happening. He doesn't seem to know how to get angry. It's the only thing I've got against him.
Female pupil: Well, I don't know about Mrs Stephens. She seems very nervous. She sort of patters on, all the time. She is always trying to seek approval, wants very much for the class to approve of her. We don't know what to do. It makes you feel embarrassed for her.
Interviewer: How do you mean, she tries to seek approval?
Pupil: She just seems to want us to approve of her. For example, she never tells you you're wrong, she just says, "Well, perhaps" or something like that. I wish she would be more . . . um, authoritarian.

Comments like this, bemoaning a lack of firmness in particular teachers, were directed at men as often as at women; and yet the pupils still seemed to hold the general preconception that men are the more effective disciplinarians. Many expressed a conviction that male teachers in general tolerate "less mucking around", and that pupils respond more readily to a rebuke or command when it comes from a man.

Female pupil: I think men probably have a securer . . . They know how to handle a class better, and you pay more attention to them. I think. I mean if someone sort of starts mucking around, they will say so, won't they? Miss Austin is quite competent, but I've had quite a few women teachers and they will let the class go. I think men can handle the class better.

Male pupil: A man would take a much stronger line. I always used to prefer women teachers to men because you could sidetrack them.

Female pupil: Some people might be more threatened by a male teacher.

Interviewer: Some girls, do you mean?

Pupil: Yes, and even boys I think. Because if a male teacher yells at you for not doing your work or not getting it in on time, I think it produces a a harsher effect. I don't think it should be like that, but that's society, isn't it?

Male pupil: Women may find it harder to get the attention of the group, and try to compensate by being more friendly, almost trying to win friends.

Although these issues cannot be resolved in the present study, one can speculate about the possible implications of pupils' preconceptions for classroom inter-action. Do pupils commonly interpret the friendliness of female teachers as an attempt to compensate for lack of power? Or, for example, are pupils likely to be more submissive with male teachers, thereby confirming their expectations of masculine authority?

Gender and teaching success

When asked to indicate which of all their current teachers are most successful on twelve different aspects of teaching performance, the teachers who were most often named, by girls as well as boys, were men. But both groups of pupils tended to designate as least successful those teachers of the other sex from themselves. The reports of boys are very decisive; there is among boys a strong consensus that male teachers are best, and female teachers, worst. Girls, on the other hand, divided both their positive and negative choices much more evenly between the men and the women who taught them. It was as if boys took a more united line than girls on their preference for male teachers and their rejection of teachers of the other sex.

Pupils' preference for male teachers is most marked with respect to the academic or pedagogic side of the teacher's role. Both boys and girls are inclined to name male teachers as the ones who: know their subject best; are most successful at getting their subject across; are most likely to give sound advice about higher education and careers; and are, all in all, most competent. Boys and girls tend to agree, furthermore, that they get more work done in classes taught by men, and that male teachers come closer to dealing fairly with all the pupils in their classes; however, the meaning which pupils give to these two latter categories deserves to be looked at more closely.

In the first place, "getting lots of work done" is usually regarded as synonymous with note-taking:

Male pupil: Mr Salisbury. We take reams of notes in his class.
Male pupil: We write the whole time!
Female pupil: It must be Mr Jensen first; we are always taking notes in his
class.

Secondly, pupils' comments when asked which teacher came closest to "dealing fairly with all pupils" seemed to equate "fairness" with a failure to acknowledge the individuality of pupils:

Female pupil: I'll put Mr Belton first, because he hardly ever sees us, so he
doesn't know anyone well.
Male pupil: He talks to the class as a whole, never to individuals. As if every-
body was the same.
Female pupil: I suppose who's most objective is somebody who doesn't know
us very well, who can't tell us apart.

These comments should serve as a warning against the pitfalls of trying to measure teacher objectivity or impartiality by means of a straightforward question; when not pinned down to a single question, pupils' judgements of teachers' fairness, it will be shown later, are in fact much more complex.

If male teachers are more favourably perceived on academic dimensions, pupils prefer teachers of their own sex when they are evaluating the interpersonal side of the teacher's role. That is, girls are inclined to name female teachers as the ones who: are more helpful; understand them best; and can most readily be consulted about personal problems. Girls report, furthermore, that they get on best with female teachers and that they have more fun in classes taught by women. Boys, on the other hand, are more likely to nominate male teachers as the ones who are most successful on all these interpersonal dimensions.

The finding that girls perceive women, but boys perceive men, as more successful teachers in interpersonal terms, is consistent with the detailed comparisons pupils made of two of their teachers, one male and one female. Most of the boys report being more involved and more relaxed in the class taught by a man; while all but one of the girls report being more attentive, more at ease and more likely to participate when they are with their female teacher. It may be the case that, much as pupils value academic competence in their teachers, the quality of the pupil's involvement in classroom interaction is more influenced by the teacher's success in interpersonal relations.

Teachers' actions and pupils' self-image

The preceding analysis has indicated some of the ways in which the evaluations pupils make of their teachers are related to the teacher's sex; it has also been suggested that while pupils perceive male teachers to be more successful in pedagogical terms, boys and girls feel more at ease with teachers of their own sex. The rest of this section will be concerned to explore, not whether female or male teachers are more favourably perceived, but which particular actions on the part of teachers enter into pupils' judgements — judgements both of the teachers, and of themselves.

The initial impressions which pupils formed of their teachers depended, by and large, on displays of individual attention from the teacher:

> *Female pupil:* She wasn't at registration, but she wrote to every one of her tutees, telling them where she was and saying she wanted to see them. It was really nice.
> *Female pupil:* I thought he was a good teacher. He knew my name right away.
> *Male pupil:* I liked him because he was doing a subject I enjoyed, and he seemed to know his subject well. But he took about a week to know our names. That's what I mean about him being remote.
> *Male pupil:* I felt an immediate liking for her. Mr Hudson introduced me to her, and she stayed to help me with form-filling and things like that.

It is not at all surprising that a teacher who treats pupils as individuals, or who is friendly and helpful on first meeting, is preferred to one who is more distant. What might astonish many teachers, however, is the degree to which the same tokens of friendliness and personal attention become important constituents of pupils' views of themselves. This became clear when I asked pupils to tell me what opinion each of their teachers held of them.

> *Male pupil:* He thinks I know quite a lot about the subject. He asks me questions, and quite often asks my opinion and things like that.
> *Female pupil:* He thinks I've got potential. That's what he told my father at Parents' Night. As a person, I think he quite likes me. In class, he asks me what I think about some things, he asks me questions.
> *Male pupil:* I think she's got me sussed as the academic waster that I am. But as a person, she appears to like me. She makes plenty of joking comments to me, and she always says I give the best excuses.
> *Female pupil:* She likes me. She seemed very keen at Open Evening to have me come to the college. It shows in class, too — she knew my name right at the beginning.
> *Female pupil:* I'm in the middle, between his favourites and the ones he despises. He doesn't talk to me, but on the other hand, he doesn't ignore everything I say.

As these quotations indicate, pupils have very limited resources upon which to draw when deciding how their teachers regard them. Homework marks are used as a guide, of course, as are any explicit judgements which the teachers may have mentioned to pupils or their parents. But small expressions of attention or concern in the classroom — as when a teacher knows (or fails to know) a pupil's name, or when the teacher asks (or fails to ask) the pupil questions — are commonly taken by pupils as evidence of teachers' interest or indifference.

It might be objected that — since pupils are scarcely likely to take teachers as their "significant others" — the opinions of their teachers matter little to them anyway. Although it is the case that parents, siblings and friends have a greater overall influence on young people than do their teachers, the effects of teachers' (apparent) judgements on their pupils should not be under-estimated. Whatever opinions pupils have of their own intellectual capacities and self-worth, there is considerable pressure from school towards re-evaluation of self as pupils move up the educational ladder. Pupils are requently urged to recognise that the intellectual demands of new areas of study are not only greater than, but different from, those of previous courses; furthermore, it is impressed upon them that they are expected to display a different range of personal and interpersonal skills — a "more mature" approach. Teachers, as the only persons who can see and are presumed competent to judge, become the arbiters of pupils' performance in both these spheres. This may be particularly so for female pupils in the light of research which suggests that girls are somewhat more dependent on adult approval than boys.

As a consequence, apparently trivial actions on the part of teachers can feed back directly into pupils' views of themselves. One pupil summed up the connection between lack of attention from her teacher, and her own self-image, in a particularly telling way:

> *Female pupil:* I think he thinks I'm pretty mediocre. *I* think I'm pretty mediocre. He never points me out of the group, or talks to me, or looks at me in particular when he's talking about things. I'm just a sort of wallpaper person.

C. Experiences of classroom interaction

Sections of the pupils' interviews were designed to elicit a picture of classroom life as seen through the eyes of the pupils. Each was asked a series of questions of the type: "Which of these pupils does the teacher pay most attention to?" In pupils' experience, it is boys who stand out vividly in classroom interaction. Despite the fact that there are almost twice as many girls as boys in the seven classes, boys' names appeared nearly two and one-half times as often as girls.

Boys are, according to the pupils' reports, four times more likely than girls to join in discussion, or to offer comments in class. They are twice as likely to demand help or attention from the teacher, and twice as likely to be seen as "model pupils".

More importantly, it seems to pupils that boys receive the lion's share of teachers' attention and regard. Boys are, on pupils' accounts:

Slightly more likely to be the pupils for whom teachers display most concern.

Twice as likely to be asked questions by teachers.

Twice as likely to be regarded by teachers as highly conscientious.

Twice as likely to be those with whom teachers get on best.

Three times more likely to be praised by teachers (and slightly more likely to be criticised).

Three times more likely to be the pupils whom teachers appear to enjoy teaching.

Five times more likely to be the ones to whom teachers pay most attention.

Looking at each of the seven classes separately, boys far exceed girls as the more prominent participants in classroom encounters in every class but one. They retain their advantage over girls (although it is slightly less pronounced) in classes taught by women, as well as those taught by men. The preponderance of boys over girls on each of these dimensions is no less marked in the reports provided by female pupils than in those provided by males — except that girls give a slight edge to classmates of their own sex when nominating model pupils, those for whom the teacher shows most concern, and those who are most frequently criticised. The implication is that *both* male and female pupils experience the classroom as a place where boys are the focus of activity and attention — particularly in the forms of interaction which are initiated by the teacher — while girls are placed on the margins of classroom life.

Separate and unequal: preferential treatment in the classroom

While discussing classroom interaction and their relationships with teachers, nearly all the pupils mentioned instances in which male teachers were, in their eyes, substantially more sympathetic or more attentive to the boys than to the girls.

Interviewer: What is Mr Fletcher's opinion of you, as far as you can tell?
Female pupil: I don't know. Because my opinion of him changed quite a lot over the year. At first I thought he was quite good, quite friendly . . . Then I really noticed that he had some favourites, and he kind of despised, which is what I feel he does, some of the people.
Interviewer: Who does he despise, do you think, in this group?
Pupil: Well, there's some girls at the back who don't say anything or don't talk, and he doesn't seem to encourage them to say anything, he just ignores them.
Interviewer: And is it those girls that you think he despises? It's quite a strong word, isn't it?
Pupil: Yes. Well, perhaps not despise. Perhaps he just looks down on them a bit, I don't know. It's just the kind of feeling you get if you're in that class.
Interviewer: That he doesn't have much respect for them?
Pupil: Yes.
Interviewer: Would he be like that with anybody quiet, do you think, or is it especially with girls.
Pupil: I don't know. It's probably because there's quite a few girls in our group, that it shows like that.
Interviewer: And who are his favourites then?
Pupil: Well there's a couple of boys who are quite sporty and he kind of jokes with them, and he lets them go off from class to play their rugby, and various things like that. And there's two boys he seems to talk to quite often outside class, and things like that.

Interviewer: Who does Mr Hurd most often direct questions to in this group?
Male pupil: I think he asks Arthur and Phil. He seems to ask all the boys a lot
actually.
Interviewer: Why is that? Why does he ask all the boys?
Pupil: I don't know. Perhaps it's because they always have something to say.
Interviewer: And the girls are more likely to be quiet?
Pupil: Yes. I guess so.

Interviewer: Who do you get on least well with, of all these teachers?
Female pupil: Mr Berger, him. I just don't know anything about him.
Interviewer: Sort of a distant figure?
Pupil: Yes. Well, he just . . . he doesn't kind of talk to anyone, he just talks
to, well. . . he tends to favour the blokes, in actual fact.
Interviewer: Why is that do you think?
Pupil: I don't know.
Interviewer: When you say "favour them", does he talk to them a lot?
Pupil: Well, he talks to them more, and he helps them a lot, and everything.
I don't know, perhaps he's scared of the girls.
Interviewer: Do you think that might be the case, that girls frighten him a
little?
Pupil: I don't know. You see, when I wanted to ask him about my essay, he
was really abrupt, and he walked off, and I thought "Great" (indignant
tone).
Interviewer: Is that one of the things that's made you more disappointed with
History, like you said before?
Pupil: Yes, because I've been working hard at History, but my marks went
down at the beginning, and now they're just staying where they were.
Obviously, I'm facing my essays the wrong way round and I wanted some
help with them. But I didn't really get it.
Interviewer: Is he like that with most of the girls, do you think?
Pupil: Well, there's a few of us that he treats pretty well the same as me.
There's some he just doesn't bother to talk to at all. And then there's two
which kind of play him up, and I think he makes fun of them. But I've
talked to other people and they think he's just quite embarrassed with
them, scared of them. That's another view.
Interviewer: With girls who play him up? He doesn't know how to deal with
them?
Pupil: Well, perhaps. At first I thought he was trying to encourage them to
make themselves look foolish, but now I don't know.

Interviewer: Who do you get on least well with, of all these teachers?
Female pupil: Well, Mr Bryant, he's a man, and you can't approach him really.
He seems to keep us girls at a distance.
Interviewer: Is that to do with his being a man?
Pupil: Yes, I think he isn't . . . Well, he may be worried about the opposite
sex, not feeling sure of himself. He doesn't know what to do with us.

Interviewer: Which of these pupils does Mrs Hertford get on best with?
Male pupil: I think Mrs Hertford does get on well with . . . Well, she gets on
better with the boys on the whole, both these teachers do. Mr York would
lean towards George and Simon and Ken. Although he's very broadminded,
he'd lean towards the boys in the class. But it's not an absolutely firm
division — he'll listen to Martha too, sometimes.

Interviewer: Who does Mr Evans pay most attention to in this group?

Female pupil: I think it's those three actually (pointing to three boys' names).
Interviewer: Why them?
Pupil: Well, perhaps they are very interested, so if we are doing something they are interested in, he'll say, "Oh, we had better ask Stephen".
Interviewer: And who does he pay least attention to, would you say?
Pupil: Well, it's Maria and Carol and Patricia, the girls.
Interviewer: Does he ask them questions, ever?
Pupil: Well, sometimes, but he tends . . . he tends to ask them as a group; he looks at them as a group. He'll just look generally in their direction. Whereas with the boys, he asks, "What do you think, Peter?", or whatever.

It should be emphasised that the passages reproduced above (and many similar statements) emerged spontaneously from pupils in the course of focussed discussions about their teachers and classmates; no initial reference was made by me to gender. In deciding what weight to attach to such comments, any statement, whether asserting or denying discrimination, which was not echoed separately by others from the same class was discounted. Statements which were independently corroborated by several pupils were taken to reflect a general sentiment on the part of the class. On this criterion — even without observational records of the classes in question — the quotations above have substantial support. The suggestion that certain male teachers tend to keep girls at a distance, while giving more attention, and especially more individual attention, to boys, was offered independently by every pupil interviewed, both female and male, in the classes concerned. In contrast, no charges of favouritism towards either sex mentioned in connection with female teachers had the backing of a second "witness"; and, it might be added, one male teacher was excluded altogether from such charges.

Boys and girls report the same actions by their teachers, but the interpretations they give to these actions can be very different. The two passages which follow (in response to the only question in the two hour pupil interviews which explicitly refers to gender), illustrate starkly how a teacher's actions can be insulting to girls, but regarded by boys as a trivial matter. Although they share the same classrooms, the experience of classroom life is clearly not the same for girls and boys.

Interviewer: Does it make any difference, do you think, that Mr Macmillan is a man and Mrs Wilson is a woman?
Female pupil: I suppose so, because you think he's a bit of a twit, at least I do. Whereas Mrs Wilson, I suppose I relate to her more because she's a woman.
Interviewer: And do you think she feels the same way, that it's easier for her to relate to girls?
Pupil: Possibly . . . No, I think it's equal actually, the way she relates to boys and girls. But take somebody like Mr Macmillan, he tends to relate better to the boys actually. When he's talking about military history or something like that he says, "I know you ladies won't like this" or something.
Interviewer: I see what you mean. You might feel a little bit as if you'd been excluded from that discussion.

Pupil: Yes, yes. I had another teacher like that at my old school actually. It was really annoying. He kept saying things like — it was in Physics — and he said, "Now if you were boys you would understand this." God, ugh! It really annoys me.

Interviewer: Does it make any difference, do you think, that Mr Macmillan is a man and Mrs Wilson is a woman?

Male pupil: Possibly, yes. I suppose the men sort of tend to . . . be a bit chauvinist, I suppose you could put it, but they do that as a joke really. Particularly Mr Macmillan. He tends to jokingly separate the two teams really. If it's a sort of social rights issue, he'll ask for the point of view of both sexes. Or he'll tease the girls that they won't understand something, say like military history. But he doesn't really concentrate on it.

Whatever the causes of what pupils take to be discriminatory behaviour on the part of their teachers — and the causes are undoubtedly complex — the consequences for pupils' views of themselves must be given serious consideration. As we saw earlier, small tokens of individual attention are important clues that pupils go by when deciding whether they are looked on with favour by their teachers. Because boys are given prominence by both male and female teachers in classroom activity, they have a far greater chance of feeling valued. Girls, on the other hand, who are less often singled out for attention in class, tend to assume (despite their good marks) that teachers hold them in low esteem. The girl who described herself as a "wallpaper person" was by no means the only one to react in this way to apparent indifference from teachers.

It is not only the self-images of *individual* pupils which are shaped by this process. The classroom is one of the few highly structured environments where adolescent girls and boys encounter one another on a regular basis, as comparative strangers. The experiences they have there are an important source of evaluations of their own, and the other, sex — of their assessments as to how successfully boys as a group, and girls as a group, match up to the demands of the adult world. When boys are more outspoken and manifestly confident — and especially when teachers take more notice of boys — pupils tend to see this as evidence that boys in general are more highly valued, and more capable, than girls.

Pupils' awareness of gender divisions

This section has been concerned to shed some light on pupils' perception of gender divisions in patterns of classroom interaction. The quantitative analysis showed clearly that pupils consider boys to be dominant, and girls to be much more marginal, in six of the seven classes concerned. Transcripts from the interviews show, furthermore, that most pupils are in regular contact with male teachers who appear, on their account, to favour boys over girls. In the light of these findings, it is instructive to look carefully at pupils' responses to the only question in their interview schedule which dealt explicitly with gender: the question, "Does it make any difference that Ms A is a woman and Mr Y is a man?"

One-third of the pupils, all boys, said "No"; but these replies were markedly inconsistent with other statements those pupils made. Most of the negative responses were contradicted by statements made earlier in the interview, and several were followed immediately by comments asserting that the sex of the teacher did, indeed, make a difference.

> *Interviewer:* Does it make any difference, do you think, that Mr Roll is a man and Mrs Murphy is a woman?
> *Male pupil:* Not really, no. I think the men tend to be more energetic than the women, but looking at it the other way Miss Gibbon is far more energetic, say, than Mr Kramer is. And I think that the men, such as Mr Kramer and Mr Roll and Mr Pierce, they are more direct, where the women are a bit more unsure of themselves . . . The women don't use the same force. Whereas Mr Roll will say, 'Do this or else', Mrs Murphy will just keep on at you, she'll just nag . . . I think that Mr Pierce is very successful with both boys and girls, whereas in the other classes . . . Well, Mr Roll doesn't seem to want to have much to do with the girls, he tends to see the boys as more . . . well, perhaps more lively, I don't know. But he is more relaxed with them, you can see that.

Half of the *affirmative* replies — "Yes, it does make a difference" — emphasised general qualities which teachers of a particular sex where observed or expected to display, rather than claims of preferential treatment to girls or to boys. Yet all but one of such replies had been preceded, earlier in the interviews, by observations about the way the treatment received by boys from their (male) teachers differed from that received by girls. One girl, for example, who had related at length early in the interview how her male teacher "concentrated more" on the boys, had only this to say in reply to the more explicit question:

> *Interviewer:* Does it make any difference, do you think, that Miss Holloway is a woman and Mr Wandsworth is a man?
> *Female pupil:* Well, yes actually. I think that Miss Holloway is much more motherly. She's just like that.

The confused pattern of responses to the explicit question may be due, in part, to ambiguity in the wording; but that ambiguity is itself the result of the attempt to formulate a question which would indicate the area of interest without putting words into pupils' mouths. It was left up to them to decide what "any difference" meant in this context.

However, apart from this ambiguity, I am inclined to think that the replies to this question illustrate a more general point: that pupils' experiences of gender differentiation in the classroom, though very real to the pupils themselves, are only partially articulated, in a way that suggests that gender divisions remain, for many of them, a largely unreflected domain. There are many cases where pupils not only report that a teacher reacts differently to the same behaviour when it is manifest by both a girl and a boy, but recognise, furthermore, that the sex of the pupil is the crucial basis of differentiation — and yet, despite this, the pupils do not appear to register it as an instance of sexual discrimination.

Interviewer: Who do you think the teacher feels most concerned about, in this group?

Female pupil: I don't know how he feels about Sarah, because she does miss a lot of lectures when she finds them boring. But I don't think he worries about her not going that much.

Interviewer: Why doesn't he worry?

Pupil: Maybe he does. But he doesn't remark when she does turn up, and he doesn't say things like 'Oh Sarah's not here again', like he does with some of the boys, when she doesn't come . . .

Interviewer: Who does he regard as being least conscientious or as wasting time?

Pupil: John Jones, when he was there. Actually, he tended to ask John a lot (of questions, referring to an earlier query from me).

Interviewer: Did he? Why was that?

Pupil: I think he liked him. I think he thought he was a bit of a lad, you know, not going to his lectures and that.

Interviewer: He found that quite amusing, then?

Pupil: I think so, yes.

Interviewer: Do you think he thinks Sarah is a bit of a lad, when she doesn't come to class?

Pupil: No, I don't think he does, I don't think he thinks anything, you know.

Interviewer: So his attitudes to John and Sarah are very different, then?

Pupil: Yes, I think so.

Interviewer: Why?

Pupil: He probably thinks, well, that's what all the young lads do, you know. And maybe he did it one time when he was young. I don't know. Because he's always made some remark on John when he did come, but it was never sarcastic, it was always quite joking.

Interviewer: As if he secretly approved of it?

Pupil: Yes, that's it.

The taken for granted quality of much of the pupils' experience of sexual differentiation — their lack, by and large, of a theoretical framework in which to locate such experiences — suggests that attempts to tap pupils' awareness of sexual divisions in the classroom by means of pre-coded questionnaires or of abstract questions could be not only unfruitful, but positively misleading.

D.   The faceless bunch: gender divisions in coeducation

It was argued earlier that the experiences boys and girls have in mixed classes contribute to their evolving views about their own, and the other, sex. When boys are more outspoken and manifestly confident — and especially when teachers take more notice of boys — pupils tend to see this as evidence that boys in general are more capable, and more highly valued, than girls.

Interviewer: Which of these pupils gets asked questions most often by the teacher?

Female pupil: Well, Terence does. And Johnny. And Mr Howard asks Rob a
lot of questions as well.
Interviewer: And which pupils join in discussions or make comments most
often?
Pupil: Rob says a lot, and Julian, and Paul, and Johnny too. They all make a
lot of noise, all those boys. That's why I think they're more intelligent
than us.

The down-grading of girls in their own eyes and those of their male classmates is
confirmed by other parts of the interviews. Both teachers and pupils ranked the
members of each class according to their success in the subject. Before comparing the rank orders made by teachers with those constructed by pupils, the
following hypotheses were set out: first, that girls would know where they
stood in relation to other girls, but would place boys higher in the rank order
than teachers had done; second, that boys would give an accurate account of the
rank order of boys, but would assign girls a lower position than teachers had
done; and third, that the net effect of pupils' "errors" would be an over-
estimation of the academic standing of boys, and an under-estimation of that of
girls. Since pupils (according to their own comments) rarely share either their
marks or judgements passed on them by teachers with pupils of the other sex,
the sexual distribution of classroom interaction is one of the few clues that girls
have for judging the performance of boys, or boys, of girls. Therefore it was
predicted that, even in cases where teachers rated the girls as more successful
than the boys, pupils would think the opposite was true.

The results support these predictions to a striking degree. In the 19 cases out
of 24 where pupils' rankings were different from those of their teachers, all of
the girls under-estimated their rank; all but one of the boys over-estimated theirs.
Furthermore, two-thirds of these errors involve only classmates of the other sex
— that is, girls down-grading themselves relative to boys, boys up-grading themselves relative to girls.

These data on pupil rankings, combined with the comments of the pupils
themselves, strongly support the contention that the prominence of boys in
classroom interaction plays an active part in the regeneration of a sexual
hierarchy, in which boys are the indisputably dominant partners. Girls appear to
boys — and more importantly, to themselves — as less capable than they "really"
are.

The devaluation of girls which is the typical consequence of interaction in
these classrooms can be, on occasion, undermined. In the first place, when girls
are forthcoming in class, boys appear to take them more seriously than before.
The pupil in the following quotation, for example, spoke well of only one girl —
Audrey — during the entire interview:

Male pupil: Audrey, hmm. Well, I'd like to classify myself as a better person
than her, but she takes a more active part in the history class. She speaks
out a lot, even though the statements are a bit, well . . . She is certainly
well read, there's no denying that.

Secondly, when pupils do have access to the marks awarded to classmates of the other sex (something which rarely happens), they are able to challenge the supposed relationship between outspokenness and ability:

> *Interviewer:* Which of these people are least like model pupils?
> *Male pupil:* Really these people here (pointing to a group of six girls). They don't say much, they don't contribute . . . On the other hand, I think a lot goes unsaid. Take, for example, Sandra, this girl here. She says very little, but I'm told on very good authority that she gets the best marks in the class. We might have lots of budding A.J.P. Taylors among those girls, but I guess I wouldn't really know about it, because I only really know George and Stan and Sebastian.

Girls in class: the faceless bunch

In the course of interviews, girls were more aware of their male classmates, and more circumspect in comments about them, than boys were about girls. Girls, for example, recognised the names of all their current classmates, male or female, but most boys had difficulty placing some of the girls. Some boys acknowledged female classmates only in ways that indicated the low opinion in which those girls were held.

> *Male pupil (sorting cards bearing classmates' names, points to several names):* A bunch of cackling girls, all of them.
> *Interviewer:* The ones that you just recognised, do you mean?
> *Pupil:* Yes. They sit at the back of the class and might as well be sucking lollipops all day.
> *Interviewer:* Do they speak out in class?
> *Pupil:* Yeah, but it's usually pretty mundane.
> *Interviewer:* Who speaks the least out of this class?
> *Pupil:* This faceless bunch.
> *Interviewer:* Ah — the reason they're faceless is, presumably, because they don't speak out?
> *Pupil:* Yeah. Also, they sit behind me, so. And also because they're stupid.
>
> *Male pupil (looking at card):* Hah, hah! Maggie!
> *Interviewer:* Why "hah hah"?
> *Pupil:* Because me and Martin were after young Maggie for weeks at the beginning of the year.
> *Interviewer:* With any success?
> *Pupil:* No. She said we were too outspoken. No, I think I'll rank myself above her.

Pupils were invited to name the classmates who most influenced them, those whom they would most wish to be like, and those with whom they compared themselves in terms of academic performance. There was a strong tendency for girls to name only girls, and boys to name only boys, in answer to these questions. On the rare occasions when boys mentioned girls among the people they would most wish to be like, they were quick to draw attention to girls' shortcomings:

Male pupil: Well, I'm very much like these three (boys) and those other three girls. But I don't think the girls have got any ambition. It would have to be a step up for me!

Boys' remarks indicated, as well, a reluctance to acknowledge girls as equals. One pupil, for example, mentioned two male classmates and one female as the pupils to whom he might compare himself in history class, but added:

Male pupil: But not so much Glenda. I think she's doing well; in fact, the teacher told me that Glenda's doing as well as me. But I wouldn't want to go and look at her essays, for instance. Not at a girl's.

Another pupil, sorting out the cards of those pupils who were better than him in History, remarked:

Male pupil: I'll put him in as well. Funny, actually, it's all boys in that pile.
Interviewer: Strange, isn't it?
Pupil: It's hard to imagine a girl that's better than me.
Interviewer: Can you imagine? Is it unusual?
Pupil: Yes, I can if I try maybe, but it *is* unusual. Rosemary — well, I don't know if she is better at History than me, but she is probably better at other subjects like English than me. I was at the same school as her for five years, so I know that.
Interviewer: So you can imagine a girl who's better than you.
Pupil: Yes, I can, but not in History.
Interviewer: Do you think History is more a man's subject, then, in a way?
Pupil: Probably, there's lots of wars in History. That's basically what it's about, why one country's greater than another. And as a rule, girls aren't so good at it.

If this young man had seen the marks of the girls in his History class, he would have discovered that, as his teacher reported, there were several girls who were performing more capably than him. But cross-sex comparison of marks is rare among these pupils, and this boy's insulation from comparison with his female classmates enables him to maintain his conviction of their inferior capacity for History.

Girls as well as boys seem wary of comparing themselves in a positive way with members of the other sex. However, as Jenny Shaw has argued,[8] boys in mixed classes may emphasise their masculinity by seeking to be as *unlike* girls as possible — in other words, by taking girls as a negative reference group. Certainly this seems to be the case in the present study. In reply to the question, "Who would you least wish to be like?", all of the boys named girls (and only girls). It must be emphasised that the characteristic of female pupils most vehemently rejected by boys is the apparent marginality of girls in classroom encounters. The term "faceless", used time and again by boys (but by none of the girls) to describe their female classmates, seems to sum up the boys' feeling that silence robs girls of any claim to individual identity and respect.

Interviewer: Who would you least wish to be like?

Male pupil: I don't know, let's see . . . (sorting through cards with names of classmates) . . . Oh, one of the faceless bunch I suppose. They seem so anonymous. Probably one of the gaggling girls, let's pick one. Linda, she's ugly. Yes, Linda.

Interviewer: Is that because she's ugly?

Pupil: No, but she just seems to be immature, she doesn't contribute much to the class. She stands for everything I dislike.

Interviewer: Considering everything, which of these pupils would you least wish to be like?

Male pupil: Well, it would have to be Cheryl, I suppose. She's sort of, well . . . anonymous, like she's not even there. I'd really rather end up like Greg or Tony (names of two boys he had said he disliked) if I had to. They are pretty objectionable, but I'd rather be one of them than be faceless like Cheryl.

It appears that the quietness of girls makes them an easy target for boys' disdain. Boys see this as a sign that girls are academically weak; they also ascribe to girls other traits, such as lack of ambition or of commitment, on the basis of their reticence in class.

Interviewer: Who does the teacher think is most conscientious in this group?

Male pupil: Well, he thinks these two are very conscientious, Mark and Ben. And these two, Stella and Eileen, they are as well. They will try and get their essays in on time, and they will work and make an effort, they read the books and so forth. They don't only work, they go to the same discos as Mark and Ben. But the boys, you see, they very much want to get on in the education system.

Interviewer: Do you mean that the girls are less ambitious than Mark and Ben?

Pupil: No, perhaps not. Well, they may end up in university, but . . . well, actually, I can't really imagine where the girls will end up. You can't really imagine that they want to *be* anything. Whereas the boys, they definitely want to get to university and to get good jobs — they make that clear.

Male pupil: I don't really know these three well, but I think I'd put them all in the same bracket, they're typical girls.

Interviewer: What's a typical girl, then?

Pupil: Well, maybe they've all got the same attitude, like they don't want to be here, but they are doing 'A' levels, so they might as well do some of the work. They would rather do 'A' levels, I guess, than go out and get a job.

Interviewer: Because you said "typical girls", do you think that's the case more often with girls than with boys?

Pupil: No. What I meant was, they are all the same. They all sit down in the back corner, and they don't say much out loud, you hardly know they are there . . . You can't really say "typical girls" anyway these days, because you'll get your head bitten off.

Although boys constitute their female classmates as a negative reference group, girls do not reciprocate. When asked whom they would least wish to be like, it is not boys, but other girls, whom girls reject. All but one of the female pupils named girls (and only girls) as the persons they would least wish to be like. The reasons they gave suggested that they were not simply adopting the standards of the boys, and disowning those members of their sex who were held by boys in contempt; on the contrary, many of the girls who were rejected by female classmates were more than ordinarily outspoken, and were condemned for "speaking out too aggressively" or "hogging the limelight".

PART III

SUMMARY AND CONCLUSION

Synopsis

In undertaking this research, I chose to focus not on achievement *per se* — not, that is, on the sexual distribution of knowledge and qualifications — but rather on the subtle ways in which classroom encounters bring to life and sustain sexual divisions. Part of that learning involves the regeneration of a gender hierarchy, in which those qualities and attributes that are associated with males are also the ones that are valued; becoming a woman means, all too often, learning to accept second place.

The central concern of the study has been then with the way in which, in pupils' experience, girls are placed on the margins of classroom encounters, and with the consequences this has for pupils' evolving images of the worth and capability of the sexes. Section A concentrates on the way teachers regard their male and female pupils. When asked to pair those of their pupils who were, in some educationally relevant way, most alike, male teachers, unlike their female colleagues, show an overwhelming tendency to select same-sex pairs; they appear to be much more attuned to dissimilarity between the sexes than to qualities which girls and boys may have in common. This implicit tendency to perceive girls and boys as discrete groups may be translated into actions which polarise the girls and boys in the classes they teach; nearly all their pupils volunteer that these male teachers play on the division of the sexes in classroom discussion, and that they are substantially more sympathetic or more attentive to the boys than the girls.

While male teachers differ from their female colleagues in the extent to which they differentiate girls from boys, all teachers — female as well as male — seem to be particularly responsive to the needs of the male pupils. Teachers' comments indicate that they more readily identify boys; when asked about first impressions of particular pupils, those who are reported as difficult to identify are, without exception, girls. If teachers are slower to identify girls, they are also less likely, later in the year, to single girls out for positive emotional involvement. From amongst their many pupils, teachers of both sexes overwhelmingly chose boys as the pupils to whom they are most attached, and those for whom they are most concerned. On the other hand, it is their female pupils whom teachers most readily reject. The greater positive involvement of teachers with their male pupils holds even when girls have a better academic record than the boys.

While teachers are concerned that neither girls nor boys should abandon their studies in order to get married or take a job, it is clear that teachers expect such disruptions more often in the case of their female pupils. Teachers have very different views of the futures awaiting their male and female pupils. Girls, even those with outstanding academic records, are expected to enter subordinate and conventionally feminine occupations, and unlike boys, are seen as immersed in domestic commitments. Only when a girl's behaviour in class sharply contradicts the retiring feminine stereotype are her teachers likely to imagine her in a career at odds with highly traditional expectations.

Section B explores some of the ways in which pupils regard their teachers. Pupils' expectations concerning teachers, and their evaluation of teachers, are linked in complex ways to the teacher's sex. Girls and boys believe male teachers to be more effective disciplinarians, even though this does not seem to be borne out by their current experience of classroom life. All pupils tend to judge their male teachers as more successful in academic and pedagogical terms — knowing their subject well, for example, and being able to put it across. But both girls and boys feel more at ease, more attentive and more able to participate in classroom activity when they are taught by teachers of their own sex.

One crucial finding to emerge is that superficially trivial tokens of personal attention from teachers are the very signs that pupils look for in deciding whether or not they are regarded with favour by their teachers. Small expressions of attention or concern — as when a teacher knows (or fails to know) a pupil's name, or when the teacher asks (or fails to ask) the pupil questions — are taken by pupils as evidence of the teacher's interest or indifference. When pupils are not singled out for attention in class, they tend to assume (in spite of good marks) that teachers hold them in low esteem. Hence the attitudes and expectations expressed by teachers in the previous section can have important consequences for the views girls and boys develop of themselves.

Section C reports on social relationships in the classroom, as they are seen through the eyes of the pupils. Both boys and girls report that many male teachers are noticeably more chummy with boys than with girls, while appearing to keep girls at a distance. Although some pupils clearly resent this, there are signs of bewilderment too in pupils' responses, and uncertainty as to whether such actions constitute cause for complaint. Girls show no hesitation, however, in expressing their indignation at jokes sometimes made by their teachers at the girls' expense — "Now I don't expect the ladies to understand this" — though such incidents, which girls find insulting, are regarded as trivial and unimportant by the boys.

In the eyes of the pupils, boys are more prominent than girls in every one of eleven areas of classroom interaction, and they are seen, in particular, to command the lion's share of teachers' attention and concern. Compared to girls, five times as many boys are named as the pupils to whom teachers pay most attention, three times as many boys as the ones who are often praised, and twice as many boys as the ones to whom teachers direct their questions. In short, boys dominate in the very areas that were earlier revealed as crucial for pupils' views of themselves; both female and male pupils experience the classroom as a place where boys are the focus of activity and interest, while the girls are relegated to the sidelines.

Section D looks more closely at the relationships of male and female classmates, and at the way their experience of classroom encounters is reflected in
views of their own and the other sex. Girls' reticence in class appears to make
them a prime target for the disdain of their male classmates; not only are boys
less able to identify female classmates, and reluctant to acknowledge them as
equals, but they seem to constitute girls as a negative reference group, rejecting
them for their quietness and their anonymity, their "facelessness". Girls, on the
other hand, express less suspicion or hostility towards boys, and more towards
members of their own sex who contravene the feminine stereotype of reticence.
To be accepted by girls, it seems, female pupils must efface themselves in front
of boys.

Pupils in these classes rarely pass their marks, or evaluations made of them by
teachers, on to members of the other sex, and so they draw upon their
experience of classroom interaction when judging the performance of the other
sex. Since the sexual distribution of interaction appears decisively weighted in
favour of boys, classroom encounters contribute to the devaluation of girls in
their own eyes and those of their male classmates. All pupils have a clear idea of
the rank order of their own sex in academic performance, but in the vast
majority of cases, girls downgrade themselves relative to boys, and boys upgrade
themselves in comparison to girls. Although the girls in this study are judged by
their teachers to be as capable as the boys, girls' marginalisation in the classroom,
and teachers' apparently lesser attentiveness to them, contribute to pupils' views
that boys are the more dominant, and capable, sex. Classroom interaction — the
way in which pupils and teachers relate to each other — does not merely transmit
beliefs about the superiority of one sex over the other, but actively serves to give
such beliefs a concrete foundation in personal experience.

Other writers have observed that there are systematic differences in the ways
that males and females make sense of their educational experience. Even when
females are successful, they harbour doubts about their own ability, and have a
sense that many aspects of achievement are beyond their grasp. This is
emphasised by Bisseret in her analysis of the careers of former university
students.[9] Not only did women, and women alone, circumscribe their achieve-
ments by reference to their sex (a very good job for a woman), but they also
described their educational careers passively in terms of choices made for them
(it was decided that I should do Lettres; I was encouraged to try for a place);
men, by contast, particularly those from upper and middle classes, saw themselves as initiators and active agents, in control of their own destinies (I knew I
was good; I decided; I chose). Among pupils in secondary school, a similar
process has been noted by Carol Dweck.[10] The successes of boys are seen (by
themselves and by others) as evidence of personal ability, while failures are
regarded only as temporary setbacks, since they are attributed either to bad luck
or lack of effort. On the other hand, girls' successes are regarded (again, by
themselves and others) as a chancy affair, the product of a lucky break or of
sheer plodding effort; their failures are taken as evidence of lack of ability. The
work of Dweck and of Bisseret suggests that, in a society where "ability" is
highly prized, whether women succeed at any academic task or whether they

fail, neither they nor others who appraise them are left with confidence in their ability, with faith in their capacity to sustain a good performance or to change a poor one.

It seems likely that the dynamic of classroom encounters contributes to this outcome. Even when girls are performing more successfully than boys, it is boys who stand out in coeducational classes. Girls appear to exist on the periphery of classroom life; their marginalisation in the classroom, and the lesser attention they receive from teachers, results in girls appearing to others — and, more importantly, to themselves — as less capable than they really are.

> *Interviewer:* And which pupils join in discussion or make comments most often?
>
> *Female pupil:* Rob says a lot, and Julian, and Paul, and Johnny too. They all make a lot of noise, all those boys. That's why I think they're more intelligent than us.

Intervention in the Classroom

How may the devaluation of female pupils in mixed classes be minimised? Whatever initial tendencies girls may have towards passivity (and boys, towards dominance) in classroom encounters, these are likely to be reinforced by the attitudes of their classmates. Girls are caught in a double-bind. Those who are most quiet in class are likely to be despised by their male classmates; while those who speak out most confidently may win the grudging respect of boys, but sacrifice the approval of members of their own sex. In deciding whether to participate, and how often or how forcefully to put their point of view, girls, it seems, are required to strike a particularly delicate balance.

Greater emphasis deserves to be placed, however, on those attitudes and actions of teachers which keep girls on the periphery of classroom activity. Teachers are (on their own accounts, and those of their pupils) concerned for boys, and attached to boys, more often than girls. They identify boys more readily than girls, and are reported to direct more questions and comments to their male pupils. Teachers of both sexes appear to permit the girls — even when they form the majority in the class — to be up-staged by the boys. In short, instead of drawing girls out, teachers in this study tend to go along with, and to reinforce the dominance of boys. A vicious circle is established: the less frequently girls are addressed, and encouraged to engage in classroom activity, the more that traditional beliefs about gender will appear to be vindicated — and the more girls are likely to be regarded as having nothing of value to communicate in the first place.

Male teachers have, on the evidence offered here, a heightened responsibility with regard to sexual divisions in the classroom. On their own accounts, men tend to differentiate more sharply between girls and boys in their attitudes and expectations than do women. Furthermore, pupils report that certain male teachers are noticeably more warm and sympathetic in their dealings with boys. In discussing what they experience as the favouritism of some male teachers towards boys, pupils often ventured to comment that male teachers experienced embarrassment or uneasiness in their relationships with girls. It is indeed possible that the age structure of teaching situations (older men dealing with younger girls; older women with younger boys) intersects with expectations about sexuality in such a way that it encourages male teachers to keep their distance from girls; in other words, if teachers wish to protect themselves from the appearance of sexual involvement with their pupils, then at present the male teacher-female pupil relationship is the one which is most likely to arouse suspicion. This may partially explain why female teachers seem to find less difficulty in expressing warmth towards pupils of the other sex than do men. But whatever the reasons for their attitudes and actions, male teachers must be encouraged to recognise (and to rectify) the damaging effects which their apparent leaning towards boys has on the class as a whole.

Discussion of the particular case of male teachers should not, however, be allowed to obscure a more central problem: why is it that teachers of both sexes are more likely to "reject" girls, while showing a greater readiness to express attachment and concern for boys? Teachers involved in this study were, on the whole, conscientious and strongly committed to the welfare of their pupils. Some of the apparent insensitivity towards girls is, it seems to me, an *unintended* consequence of the guidelines teachers adopt when deciding how they will distribute, amongst their many pupils, their limited time and attention. Three major criteria for distinguishing "deserving" pupils were mentioned by teachers in this study. Teachers felt that pupils who are trying hard, those who display outstanding ability, or pupils who are obviously experiencing difficulties with their work, should have first claim on their energies. On the surface, these criteria of commitment, talent and need may seem to be reasonable; but all three intersect with the initial reticence of girls in class so as to favour the choice of boys, rather than girls, as objects of the teacher's attention and concern.

The process by which teachers identify pupils with commitment, talent or need is problematic, involving evaluations of oral as well as written contributions. For example (as the teacher quoted below points out), it is easy to underestimate the commitment of a pupil who completes assignments adequately but who says little about the amount of effort expended:

> *Interviewer:* So, to sum up what you just said, the attitude you take towards pupils who are finding the course a bit difficult varies according to how deeply the pupil is committed to the subject?
> *Female teacher:* Yes. But I think commitment is very hard to judge. Because, to a degree, your perception of commitment depends on the noise a pupil makes. A quiet, hard-working pupil may not appear to be very committed, because all the effort goes on behind the scenes.

If girls speak less in class, they have fewer opportunities than boys for displaying either 'need' or 'talent' to their teachers. On the one hand, as long as a girl's written work is adequate, teachers are likely to assume that she understands the topic; confusions and misunderstandings which may be glossed over in her written work will go undetected and unresolved, while a boy with a similar level of comprehension is more likely to have his problems noted — and worked on — in the course of class discussions. On the other hand, the impression teachers gain of a "merely competent" female pupil from looking at written work is less likely to be offset by judgments of "perceptive and original" commentary in class. There is less chance that girls will impress their teachers with the gap between written and oral expression — and more chance that a girl who writes passable essays will be assumed to be working "up to capacity".

In short, the criteria according to which teachers divide their energies among their many pupils would seem to have the *unintended* consequence of dis-advantaging the girls. These criteria may constitute a form of indirect discrimin-ation. Where teachers err in their judgments about female pupils, it is likely to be in the direction of underestimating girls' talent, their commitment and their needs. This tendency is illustrated in a view of female pupils that was expressed by teachers on several occasions: that of the 'schoolgirl', able to follow instruc-tions, but not capable of, or interested in, breaking new ground.

> *Interviewer:* Which two of those three pupils are most alike?
> *Male teacher:* Penny and Anna. They're standard school-leaver young ladies, of no great difference in social background. Well, some difference in social background, but schoolgirls in their attitude . . . adequate, but no out-standing ability.

There are two important consequences of the priorities of teachers which have been discussed here. First, though it need not be the case that teachers grade girls more harshly than their present performance warrants, female pupils are less likely to be challenged and stretched academically, with serious implications for their *future* performance. Second, girls are less likely than boys to be singled out as worthy recipients of the teacher's attention; this (quite apart from its academic consequences) makes girls feel less valued in the classroom, and reinforces other pressures urging them to take a back seat in classroom activity.

The attitudes and orientations of teachers which may inform their classroom behaviour represent only one half of the equation; the other relevant con-sideration is pupils' initiatives, and the ways in which teachers may respond. Some writers have argued that male pupils place greater demands on teachers — demands in the form of questions, comments, gestures which invite attention or disruptive activity — and that teachers' greater attention to boys may be partially a straightforward response to these immediate "pupil presses". If it is the case that teachers are faced with such demands from boys more than from girls (and the pupils in this study seemed to think it to be so), they have two options other than outright acquiescence.

In the first place, teachers should make a conscious effort to channel more of their attention and energies to quieter pupils — to those who, like 'Edith' in the following quote, do not put themselves forward in class:

> *Interviewer:* Who, all in all, does Mrs. Symonds pay most attention to in this group?

Male pupil: She pays a lot of attention to Bob and me. Steve gets a lot of attention. And Tristan.

Interviewer: Who gets paid least attention, do you think, in this class?

Pupil: Edith, I think. She gets least attention in Mr. Morgan's class as well. Then there's those other two girls, Judy and Eve. Those three, they are very quiet, they don't say very much. They are just bumbling along so they get left alone. Well, perhaps that's not quite right. Edith, she's touch and go, but the other two are more intelligent, they are just quiet . . .

Interviewer: Who does Mrs. Symonds seem most concerned about in this group?

Pupil: I think Mrs. Symonds is a bit worried about me, and about Steve and Tristan, because we miss classes a lot. She mentions it in a roundabout way, and seems concerned. I don't think she worries much about the others, about Edith and Judy and Eve, say.

Interviewer: Even though they are very quiet?

Pupil: Judy and Eve are quite competent. But Edith, I don't think she can handle it, I don't think she understands what's going on.

Interviewer: It's strange, though, that if Edith doesn't know what she's doing, that the teacher doesn't worry about her.

Pupil: Yeah, but you just completely don't notice Edith. You just forget her existence. Whereas if me or Steve or Bob or Tristan are away, Mrs. Symonds notices that, because we usually make a lot of noise in class.

Though there are some quiet boys in secondary classrooms, the neglect of quiet pupils works, on the whole, to the disadvantage of girls.

Secondly (and more fundamentally), if girls do make fewer demands than boys, teachers could give a higher priority to re-shaping the sexual distribution of interaction in the classroom. We have seen that pupils place a considerable significance on what might otherwise be trivial aspects of social relations in the classroom — on being singled out of the group, having one's name known, being addressed individually: such actions could be taken account of by teachers in an effort to create an atmosphere in which girls (and other reticent pupils) can more readily participate. As has been demonstrated in linguistic experiments, fluency is very much dependent on social context: children who confine themselves to monosyllabic answers in situations they see as threatening may become extremely talkative and articulate when placed in more congenial surroundings, with an obviously sympathetic adult. It is, arguably, only when teachers create an atmosphere in which girls and boys are (and know themselves to be) equally valued and equally welcome, that girls will be positively encouraged to voice their opinions and ideas.

A reluctance on the part of teachers to bring girls more to the forefront in classroom activity may be based on at least two grounds: a concern not to embarrass or cause distress to timid pupils by putting them on the spot; and a commitment to non-interference with "normal" patterns of classroom interaction. Both these grounds are open to question.

In the first instance, the potential embarrassment to timid pupils which may in some cases result from being "put on the spot" may be outweighed by the constant undermining of confidence that stems from being (apparently) ignored. Moreover, the notion that reticent pupils will shrink under the direct gaze of the teacher may sometimes contain an element of myth which, if untested, will simply force those pupils to remain in the shadows — as one teacher discovered in a telling example:

> *Interviewer:* Would you describe Martin as outspoken or reticent in class?
> *Female teacher:* Well, I would have described him as exceptionally reticent, for a boy. He hardly ever said a word; and I was worried that if I leaned on him too hard, he might be embarrassed and withdraw. But you see, all that's changed since the conversation with his father.
> *Interviewer:* How's that?
> *Teacher:* Well since his father said he wasn't shy, since that time, I've made a point of trying to make Martin speak. And in fact, in the several times I've seen him since then, he has made a contribution.
> *Interviewer:* How did the change occur?
> *Teacher:* Well, it was very simple really. I've looked at him directly when I posed a problem, or just outright asked his opinion. Somewhat to my surprise, he responded right away. When I just direct a comment at the group, though, he won't offer any comment.

The attempt to engage less forthcoming pupils requires both ingenuity and effort on the part of teachers; there are no ready-made solutions. But just as teachers seek ways of encouraging students to improve their capacity for written expression — and as many manage to do so without causing undue embarrassment — so too it should be possible for concerned teachers to create for girls a more central place in classroom life.

As for the commitment to "non-interference", I would argue that intervention in the learning process, aimed at encouraging the development of pupils in valued directions, is (almost by definition) a fundamental part of teachers' responsibilities. Participation in classroom activities *is* valued; it enters into pupils' assessments of the relative capacities of themselves and their male and female classmates, and may influence teachers' judgements of the needs and abilities of girls and boys. It would seem both illogical and unjust if, on the one hand, reticence in the classroom "counted against" a pupil but, on the other hand, teachers regarded the encouragement of participation as an illegitimate sphere for intervention. Toleration by teachers of practices which reinforce the devaluation of girls in their own eyes and those of their classmates, contributes directly to maintenance of the status quo: non-intervention (as much as intervention) constitutes a significant political act.

A parallel may be drawn with Bernstein's observations about the discontinuities between past and present faced by working class children entering primary school; such children are in a difficult position, he argues, because they have not only to learn new things, but also, more importantly, to unlearn patterns of interaction that have been established in earlier contexts.[11] Similarly, the teachers interviewed in this study were very anxious that pupils should realise that Advanced level study is different in quality from anything that preceded it — requiring analysis rather than description, originality of style rather than rote recitation of facts, and so on. It may be that the quiet conformism to which many girls are so effectively groomed in earlier years is suddenly in the view of 'A' level teachers, deemed inappropriate; if this is the case, and girls are having to unlearn patterns of behaviour they learned earlier, then it is reasonable to expect that teachers will give them firm and explicit guidance in the process of re-socialisation.

CONCLUSION

Equal rights legislation alone is no guarantee of equality. The enactment of the Sex Discrimination Act makes it all the more urgent that we give close scrutiny to the internal workings of schools — that we unravel and transcend the more subtle processes by which girls are taught to be women, and boys to be men. Encounters in coeducational establishments will, under conditions of formal equality, play a potent part in reinforcing and legitimating the subordination of women in personal, economic and political life, as long as such encounters continue to bring to life and sustain sexual divisions.

Girls may follow the same curriculum as boys — may sit side by side with boys in classes taught by the same teachers — and yet emerge from school with the implicit understanding that the world is a man's world, in which women can and should take second place. To undermine this dynamic would be to make pupils aware of the possibility of the dismantling of sexual divisions. The transformation of pupils' consciousness — enabling them to have confidence in their capacity to alter the course of their own lives — is and must be an important step in the process of social transformation.

Postscript

If I were writing a fresh version of *Gender and Schooling* today, drawing on our experience of sexism in education since the passing of the Sex Discrimination Act, I would want to make three additional arguments. First, I would emphasise the importance of positive action programmes. In order to overhaul a curriculum that has for generations devalued women and their concerns; in order to persuade girls that jobs in engineering and technology are open to them, when the experience of their mothers and sisters and friends (indeed, of the occupational structure itself) tells them differently; in order to move from a situation of male privilege towards one of greater equality, we need to channel more resources towards girls than ever before. It is not enough to aim merely for *equal* educational provision, when girls' education labours under the handicap of generations of disadvantage.

Second, I would stress the importance of establishing back-up facilities, so that individual teachers less often have to struggle on their own with the difficult problems thrown up by sexism in education: facilities such as resources centres which pool the efforts of teachers and full-time researchers to create more exciting and accurate teaching materials; and working parties within each school to monitor progress towards equal opportunities, to formulate guidelines for good practice and to deal with complaints.

Third, I would stress the importance of direct confrontation with sexism within education. We owe it to girls to help them understand that their individual experience of sexism, inside and outside school, is not unique. We could consider making a space for girls-only groups within mixed schools, where girls could share experiences and work out for themselves constructive ways of dealing with gender inequality and sexual harassment. We also need to work with boys, to help them reflect on the meaning of masculinity and on the effects of their behaviour on girls. Some teachers shrink from discussion of gender divisions, claiming that the schools' responsibility for equal opportunities extends only to achievement — to, for example, persuading more girls to continue with the study of mathematics. But attainment cannot justifiably be separated in this way from the understanding of gender inequality. We cannot enact a commitment to enabling girls to fulfill their potential in terms of skills and qualifications, without also encouraging them to reflect upon the ways in which women's lives have been circumscribed, and the ways that they might be transformed.

References for postscript

Positive action programmes are considered in: Sadie Roberts, Anna Coote and Elizabeth Ball, *Positive Action for Women: the Next Step*, National Council for Civil Liberties (1981).

Examples of the successes of working parties dealing with equal opportunities, and of good practice in schools, as well as concise summaries of recent research are contained in: Equal Opportunities Commission, *Research Bulletin No. 6, Spring 1982*, subtitled 'Gender and the secondary school curriculum', available free of charge from: Carolyn Orry, Publicity Section, Equal Opportunities Commission, Overseas House, Quay Street, Manchester M3 3HN.

NOTES

1. The statistics cited in the previous section can be found in: Office of Population Censuses and Surveys, Social Survey Division, *The General Household Survey 1977*; Department of Education and Science (DES), Statistics of Education 1977, Vol. 2, *School Leavers CSE and GCE*; DES, Statistics of Education 1976, Vol. 3, *Further Education*; DES et al, *Education Statistics for the United Kingdom*, 1976 and 1977; Jean Coussins, "Equality for women: have the laws worked?", *Marxism Today* (January 1980); *Department of Employment Gazette*, Vol. 88, No. 2 (February 1980).

2. For those interested in exploring the question of gender differences in aptitudes, L.D. Edwards' paper, "Girls and mathematics: why don't they mix?", available from the Equal Opportunities Commission, is a useful starting point, as is D. Tresemer, "Assumptions made about gender roles" in M. Millman and R. Kanter (eds) *Another Voice*, Anchor Books (1975).

3. Science textbooks are not, of course, the only teaching materials that marginalise girls and women. Content analysis of reading schemes and children's literature in general have demonstrated that the portrayal of females tends to be restricted to the role of domestic helpmeets; girls and women are, it seems (whether as sisters, daughters or mothers), the ones intended by the phrase "they also serve who only stand and wait". Females are also less visible in this literature than males; analysing British reading schemes in use in the 1970's, Glenys Lobban found that male central characters outnumbered females by a ratio of 5 to 1. The problem is not only that these books fail to challenge the sexual division of labour in the real world; they are, as Lobban commented, more sexist than reality.

    Studies of children's literature include: G. Lobban, "Sex-roles in reading schemes", *Educational Review*, Vol. 27, No. 3; C. Nightingale, "Sex roles in children's literature" in S. Allen, L. Sanders and J. Wallis (eds) *Conditions of Illusion*, Feminist Books (1974); Northern Women's Group's Education Study Group, "Sex-role learning: a study of infant readers" in M. Wandor (ed) *The Body Politic* (1972); Children's Rights Workshop (eds) *Sexism in Children's Books*, Writers and Readers Publishing Co-operative (1976); B. Dixon, *Catching Them Young I: Sex, Race and Class in Children's Fiction*, Pluto Press (1977).

4. The research mentioned here is discussed in Casey Miller and Kate Swift, *Words and Women*, Pelican (1979), Chapter 2. The quotation is from page 39. Many other examples of sexist language, and ways of altering it, are available in "The McGraw-Hill Guidelines", in Children's Rights Workshop (eds) *Sexism in Children's Books*, Writers and Readers Publishing Co-operative (1976).

5. For those who wish to have further details of the research techniques and design, copies of the dissertation in which the research is fully written up — entitled *Gender and the Classroom: a Study of Male and Female Views of Classroom Life* — are available in the WRRC, and also in the libraries of the University of Essex, and the Institute of Education, London.

    To protect the privacy of the teachers and pupils who participated in the research, all names offered in quotations are fictitious.

6. Articles and books mentioned in this introduction are, in order of their appearance:
    — A.H. Halsey, A.F. Heath and J.M. Ridge, *Origins and Destinations*, Clarendon Press (1980).
    — M. Young, *The Rise of the Meritocracy*, Penguin (1961).

— C. Dyhouse, "Good wives and little mothers: social anxieties and the school-girls' curriculum" in *Oxford Review of Education*, Vol. 3, No. 1 (1977); and "Darwinistic ideas and the development of women's education in England" in *History of Education*, Vol. 5, No. 1, (1976).

— A. Davin, "Mind that you do as you are told: reading books for Board School girls, 1870-1902" in *Feminist Review*, No. 3 (1979).

— Central Advisory Council for Education, *Half Our Future* (Newsom Report), HMSO (1963).

— T. Blackstone and H. Weinreich-Haste, "Why are there so few women scientists and engineers?", *New Society* (21 February 1980).

— R. Kelsall, A. Poole and A. Kuhn, *Six Years After*, Sheffield University Press, Sheffield (1970).

— J. Shaw, "Sexual Divisions in the classroom" in *Teaching Girls to be Women*, Mimeo, University of Essex (1977).

— S. Sharpe, *Just Like a Girl: How Girls Learn to be Women*, Pelican (1976).

— N. Bisseret, *Education, Class Language and Ideology*, Routledge & Kegan Paul (1979).

— S. Bowles and H. Gintis, *Schooling in Capitalist America*, Routledge & Kegan Paul (1976).

— A.M. Wolpe, "Education and the sexual division of labour" in A. Kuhn and A.M. Wolpe (eds) *Feminism and Materialism*, Routledge & Kegan Paul (1978).

— R. Deem, *Women and Schooling*, Routledge & Kegan Paul (1978).

— M. David, "The family-education couple: towards an analysis of the William Tyndale dispute" in G. Littlejohn et al (eds) *Power and the State*, Croom Helm (1978).

— A. McRobbie, "Working class girls and the culture of femininity" in Women's Study Group, CCCS, *Women Take Issue*, Hutchinson (1978).

— J. Okely, "Privileged, schooled and finished: boarding education for girls" in S. Ardener (ed) *Defining Females*, Croom Helm (1978).

— J. Westergaard and H. Resler, *Class in a Capitalist Society*, Heinemann (1975).

— E. Byrne, *Women and Education*, Tavistock (1978).

— Department of Education and Science, *Curricular Differences for Boys and Girls*, Education Survey 21, HMSO (1975).

— J. Shaw, "Sexual divisions in the classroom" in *Teaching Girls to be Women*, Mimeo, University of Essex (1977).

— J. Shaw, "Finishing school: some implications of sex-segregated education" in D.L. Barker and S. Allen (eds) *Sexual Divisions and Society*, Tavistock (1976).

— C. Benn and B. Simon, *Half Way There*, Penguin (1972).

— H. Weinreich-Haste and A. Kelly, "Science is for girls?", paper presented to the British Association for Advancement of Science (1978); A. Kelly, "Science for men only?", *New Scientist* (29 August 1974).

— A.M. Wolpe, *Some Processes in Sexist Education*, WRRC (1977).

— B. Bernstein, *Class, Codes and Control*, Vol. 3, Routledge & Kegan Paul (1975).

— P. Bourdieu and J.-C. Passeron, *Reproduction in Education, Society and Cul* Sage (1977).

— N. Keddie, "Classroom knowledge" in M.F.D. Young (ed) *Knowledge and Control*, Collier-MacMillan (1971).

— L. Davies, "The contribution of the secondary school to the sex typing of girls", unpublished M.Ed. dissertation, University of Birmingham, reported in L. Davies and R. Meighan, "A review of schooling and sex roles" in R. Meighan and J. Doherty (eds) *Education and Sex Roles*, special issue of

Educational Review, Vol. 27, No. 3 (June 1975).
— Carol Dweck, paper given at Cambridge Conference on sex differentiation and schooling (January 1980) and reported in T. Blackstone and H. Weinreich-Haste, "Why are there so few women scientists and engineers?", *New Society* (February 21, 1980).

7. N. Keddie, "Classroom knowledge" in M.F.D. Young (ed) *Knowledge and Control*, Collier-MacMillan (1971).

8. J. Shaw, "Sexual divisions in the classroom" in *Teaching Girls to be Women*, Mimeo, University of Essex (1977).

9. N. Bisseret, *Education, Class Language and Ideology*, Routledge & Kegan Paul (1979).

10. C. Dweck, paper given at Cambridge conference on sex differentiation and education, (January 1980); cited in T. Blackstone and H. Weinreich-Haste, "Why are there so few women scientists and engineers?", *New Society* (February 21, 1980).

11. B. Bernstein, *Class, Codes and Control*, Vol. 1, Routledge & Kegan Paul (1971).

BIBLIOGRAPHY

BISSERET, N. *Education, Class Language and Ideology*, Routledge & Kegan Paul (1979).

BYRNE, E. *Women and Education*, Tavistock (1978).

DAVIES, L. and MEIGHAN, R. "A review of schooling and sex roles, with particular reference to the experience of girls in secondary schools" in R. Meighan and J. Doherty (eds) *Education and Sex Roles* (Special issue of *Educational Review*, Vol. 27, No. 3, June 1975).

DEEM, R. *Women and Schooling*, Routledge & Kegan Paul (1978)

DEEM, R. (ed) *Schooling for Women's Work*, Routledge & Kegan Paul (1980)

FRAZIER, N. and SADKER, M. *Sexism in School and Society*, Harper & Row

GOOD, T., SIKES, N. and BROPHY, J. "Effects of teacher sex and student sex on classroom interaction" in *Journal of Educational Psychology*, Vol. 65, No. 1 (1973).

HANNON, V. *Ending Sex-Stereotyping in Schools: a Sourcebook for School-based Teacher Workshops*, Equal Opportunities Commission (1980).

LIGHTFOOT, S. "Sociology of education: perspectives on women" in M. Millman and R. Kanter (eds) *Another Voice*, Anchor Books (1975).

LOBBAN, G. "The influence of the school on sex-role stereotyping" in J. Chetwynd and O. Hartnett (eds) *The Sex Role System*, Routledge & Kegan Paul (1978).

MACCOBY, E. and JACKLIN, C. *The Psychology of Sex Differences*, Oxford University Press (1975).

MARKS, P. "Femininity in the classroom: an account of changing attitudes" in J. Mitchell and A. Oakley (eds) *The Rights and Wrongs of Women*, Penguin (1976).

SHARPE, S. *Just Like a Girl*, Pelican (1976).

SHAW, J. "Finishing school: some implications of sex-segregated education" in D. L. Barker and S. Allen (eds) *Sexual Divisions and Society*, Tavistock (1976).

SPENDER, D. and SARAH, E. (eds) *Learning to Lose*, The Women's Press (1980).

TEACHING GIRLS TO BE WOMEN, Collection of papers given at conference at University of Essex, mimeograph (1977).

WEINER, G. "Education and the Sex Discrimination Act", *Educational Research*, Vol. 20, No. 3.

WILLIS, P. *Learning to Labour*, Saxon House (1977).

WOLPE, A.-M. "The official ideology of girls' education" in M. Flude and J. Ahier (eds) *Educability, Schools and Ideology*, Croom Helm (1975).

WOLPE, A.-M. *Some Processes in Sexist Education*, WRRC (1977).